HYDROGEN—ITS PRODUCTION AND ENERGY USES

HEARING

BEFORE THE

SUBCOMMITTEE ON ENERGY RESEARCH AND PRODUCTION

AND THE

SUBCOMMITTEE ON ENERGY DEVELOPMENT AND APPLICATIONS

OF THE

COMMITTEE ON SCIENCE AND TECHNOLOGY U.S. HOUSE OF REPRESENTATIVES

NINETY-SIXTH CONGRESS

SECOND SESSION

JUNE 25, 1980

I0130140

[No. 174]

Printed for the use of the
Committee on Science and Technology

Books for Business
New York-Hong Kong

Hydrogen-Its Production and Energy Uses

by
U. S. House of Representatives Committee on
Science and Thechnology

ISBN: 0-89499-071-3

Reprinted from the 1981 edition

Books for Business
New York - Hong Kong
http://www.BusinessBooksInternational.com

COMMITTEE ON SCIENCE AND TECHNOLOGY

DON FUQUA, Florida, *Chairman*

ROBERT A. ROE, New Jersey
MIKE McCORMACK, Washington
GEORGE E. BROWN, JR., California
JAMES H. SCHEUER, New York
RICHARD L. OTTINGER, New York
TOM HARKIN, Iowa
JIM LLOYD, California
JEROME A. AMBRO, New York
MARILYN LLOYD BOUQUARD, Tennessee
JAMES J. BLANCHARD, Michigan
DOUG WALGREN, Pennsylvania
RONNIE G. FLIPPO, Alabama
DAN GLICKMAN, Kansas
ALBERT GORE, JR., Tennessee
WES WATKINS, Oklahoma
ROBERT A. YOUNG, Missouri
RICHARD C. WHITE, Texas
HAROLD L. VOLKMER, Missouri
DONALD J. PEASE, Ohio
HOWARD WOLPE, Michigan
NICHOLAS MAVROULES, Massachusetts
BILL NELSON, Florida
BERYL ANTHONY, JR., Arkansas
STANLEY N. LUNDINE, New York
ALLEN E. ERTEL, Pennsylvania
KENT HANCE, Texas

JOHN W. WYDLER, New York
LARRY WINN, JR., Kansas
BARRY M. GOLDWATER, JR., California
HAMILTON FISH, JR., New York
MANUEL LUJAN, JR., New Mexico
HAROLD C. HOLLENBECK, New Jersey
ROBERT K. DORNAN, California
ROBERT S. WALKER, Pennsylvania
EDWIN B. FORSYTHE, New Jersey
KEN KRAMER, Colorado
WILLIAM CARNEY, New York
ROBERT W. DAVIS, Michigan
TOBY ROTH, Wisconsin
DONALD LAWRENCE RITTER,
   Pennsylvania
BILL ROYER, California

HAROLD P. HANSON, *Executive Director*
PHILIP B. YEAGER, *General Counsel*
REGINA A. DAVIS, *Administrator*
PAUL A. VANDER MYDE, *Minority Staff Director*

SUBCOMMITTEE ON ENERGY RESEARCH AND PRODUCTION

MIKE McCORMACK, Washington, *Chairman*

MARILYN LLOYD BOUQUARD, Tennessee
ROBERT A. ROE, New Jersey
STANLEY N. LUNDINE, New York
ROBERT A. YOUNG, Missouri
RICHARD C. WHITE, Texas
HOWARD WOLPE, Michigan
RONNIE G. FLIPPO, Alabama
NICHOLAS MAVROULES, Massachusetts
RICHARD L. OTTINGER, New York
BERYL ANTHONY, JR., Arkansas

JOHN W. WYDLER, New York
EDWIN B. FORSYTHE, New Jersey
TOBY ROTH, Wisconsin
BARRY M. GOLDWATER, JR., California
MANUEL LUJAN, JR., New Mexico
HAROLD C. HOLLENBECK, New Jersey

SUBCOMMITTEE ON ENERGY DEVELOPMENT AND APPLICATIONS

RICHARD L. OTTINGER, New York, *Chairman*

JAMES J. BLANCHARD, Michigan
DOUG WALGREN, Pennsylvania
DAN GLICKMAN, Kansas
ALBERT GORE, JR., Tennessee
ROBERT A. YOUNG, Missouri
RICHARD C. WHITE, Texas
HAROLD L. VOLKMER, Missouri
HOWARD WOLPE, Michigan
NICHOLAS MAVROULES, Massachusetts
BILL NELSON, Florida
BERYL ANTHONY, JR., Arkansas
ALLEN E. ERTEL, Pennsylvania
KENT HANCE, Texas
ROBERT A. ROE, New Jersey
MIKE McCORMACK, Washington

HAMILTON FISH, JR., New York
KEN KRAMER, Colorado
WILLIAM CARNEY, New York
DONALD LAWRENCE RITTER,
   Pennsylvania
ROBERT W. DAVIS, Michigan
JOHN W. WYDLER, New York
ROBERT K. DORNAN, California
ROBERT S. WALKER, Pennsylvania

CONTENTS

WITNESSES

(III)

HYDROGEN—ITS PRODUCTION AND ENERGY USES

WEDNESDAY, JUNE 25, 1980

U.S. HOUSE OF REPRESENTATIVES,
COMMITTEE ON SCIENCE AND TECHNOLOGY,
SUBCOMMITTEE ON ENERGY RESEARCH AND PRODUCTION,
SUBCOMMITTEE ON ENERGY DEVELOPMENT AND APPLICATIONS,
Washington, D.C.

The subcommittees met in joint session, pursuant to notice, at 1:37 p.m., in room 2318, Rayburn House Office Building, Hon. Richard L. Ottinger, chairman of the Energy Development and Applications Subcommittee, presiding.

Mr. OTTINGER. Today the Subcommittee on Energy Development and Applications, which I chair, is joining with the Subcommittee on Energy Research and Production, which the gentleman from Washington, Mr. McCormack, chairs—he will be with us shortly—to hold what I consider very important hearings on hydrogen production and the possibility of the use of hydrogen in meeting our Nation's energy supply needs.

There is growing awareness in the public and scientific communities that hydrogen may be a fuel with many useful applications in transporting and storing energy derived from solar, hydro, nuclear, or coal systems. For example, if hydrogen can be economically produced by using one of these plentiful energy supplies to cleave water, it is one of the most exciting fuels for the future—infinitely abundant, transportable, storable, and completely clean, the only products of reaction being water and energy.

The use of hydrogen in our society is not new. Hydrogen is a major industrial feedstock. Nearly 1 quad of hydrogen energy is already being manufactured in the United States for use in the preparation of energy intensive materials, namely, ammonia for fertilizer and additional hydrocarbons for petrochemicals.

The use of hydrogen as a fuel is in its infancy, however. The reason is that the technology for separation of hydrogen is still energy inefficient and expensive. Hydrogen is not an energy source. It must be isolated with use of other energy sources. Furthermore, hydrogen is presently being made almost totally from light hydrocarbons, such as natural gas, which are in themselves excellent energy sources and are nonrenewable. Using hydrogen fuel from such sources would not have a positive impact on energy supply. To be practical as a fuel, new hydrogen production technologies must emerge; for example, electrolysis, in which electricity splits water to hydrogen and oxygen, or the chemical reaction of coal and steam to liberate hydrogen.

I look forward to hearing the testimony of our distinguished witnesses. We have Congressman Grassley, and two panels of people who are well qualified and who have been working in this field. I am interested in how they see hydrogen as part of our energy supply system and what new and improved methods are being developed that might reduce the cost of making hydrogen from water.

I would like to welcome our first witness, my colleague, Mr. Charles Grassley, who has authored a bill, the Hydrogen Fuel Development and Use Act of 1979, H.R. 5399. I commend him for his efforts and we look forward to hearing his testimony.

Without objection—and I see that there is nobody objecting—these procedings are being recorded for the Public Broadcasting System.

STATEMENT OF HON. CHARLES E. GRASSLEY

Mr. GRASSLEY. Thank you, Mr. Chairman. I want to thank you and the committee for bringing up this issue of hydrogen as a viable energy alternative. Hydrogen will be the beginning of turning the dreams of all mankind into the reality of energy independence. Let's assure everybody, though, that we are going to explore energy alternatives in all their forms at a price which is reasonable and fair, that is renewable in nature to the greatest extent possible, and is as free as can humanly be expected from harming our environment, not only for this generation but for generations to come.

As supplies of crude oil diminish and prices get higher, we must begin to question whether we are doing the most that we can to find another source of fuel to heat our homes and fuel our vehicles. More importantly, we should be asking ourselves, is there any renewable source of energy right here in this country that might help stop the hemorrhaging of dollars of the OPEC nations. I respectfully submit to you that I believe the answer to this question is an emphatic yes. We have the power to tap coal shale, tar sands, nuclear power, solar power, and various agricultural products for making gasohol, methanol, and ethanol to generate electricity and produce vehicular fuel. However, just as important, and maybe more important, is the topic we are here to discuss today, that of hydrogen.

On September 25 last year, I introduced the first comprehensive piece of legislation ever introduced in this Congress which provides for the research, development, production, and use of hydrogen as an alternative fuel. This bill also amends the Internal Revenue Code to encourage the production and use of hydrogen as a fuel. The bill provides for tax incentives for hydrogen production and for certain equipment which uses hydrogen. Residential and business are also provided for in the bill. The bill provides for guaranteed loans not to exceed 90 percent of the aggregate cost with full payment not to exceed 20 years. It also provides for price of purchase guarantees and such other assistance as the Secretary is authorized by law to provide.

This bill specifically addresses the production of hydrogen by coal gasification or lignite, peat, and residual oil; also by ocean thermal energy conversion, by electrolytic means, by low head hydroelectric, by solar, and by other means as the Secretary of Energy deems necessary.

I fully realize that there may be other means available, such as fusion, which I also believe is familiar and the Secretary should be encouraged to pursue. Some of the potential uses of hydrogen that I see for the future are:

One, a mixture of hydrogen with natural gas. It is my understanding that we can presently add up to 15 percent hydrogen into existing natural gas pipelines with no adverse effect;

Two, for the fueling for rail and air transportation and such special applications as well as forklift trucks, mining and agricultural equipment, buses, fleet vehicles, and other multipassenger vehicles designed for short distance travel.

Three, hydrogen fuel cells for power generation; and,

Four, hydrogen used to produce ammonia rather than natural gas used to make chemical fertilizers.

In other words, hydrogen could be used to heat and cool our homes, cook our meals, and provide a fuel to power almost every type of vehicular transportation. It could reduce consumption of natural gas, which is a nonrenewable source of energy, thereby making sure we have sufficient quantities of energy for our petrochemical industries and industries for making agricultural fertilizer as well as other types of industry which rely upon natural gas.

Mr. Chairman, I have worked with many people in the scientific, educational, industrial, and governmental communities in drafting H.R. 5399. My conversations with them lead me to believe that the potential realization of this alternative energy source is far from being realized. In Provo, Utah, it is my understanding that a complete hydrogen homestead is in operation. I've seen for myself a Dodge Omni powered by hydrogen, and a bus is running in Riverside, Calif., on this fuel.

It is also my understanding that one of our major aircraft manufacturers is in the planning stages of building aircraft to fly on hydrogen. We have been in contact with people like the Billings Energy Corp., General Electric, Teledyne Corp., Johns Hopkins University, Jet Propulsion Laboratory, Westinghouse, Air Products & Chemical, Inc., Rockwell, Monsanto, United Technologies, Marion Works, Consumers Solar Electric, and many others who are presently doing work in this field already or who are presently contemplating doing more if government will show a little bit of leadership in this area. It has also been brought to my attention that several oil companies are doing research in this field as well.

The unfortunate part in all of this is that the administration has not seen fit to place a stronger emphasis in the field of research and development of hydrogen. In fact, we've seen a steady decrease in the level of funding. The only encouraging part of all this is that we have sent letters to the conferees on the synfuel bill, asking them to include hydrogen in the terminology of synthetic fuels. As you are aware, the conferees did include hydrogen in the compromise.

As a result, we must use this first step here today as a pivotal point since hydrogen was included in that bill only to a limited degree. Recently the National Research Council issued a report entitled "Hydrogen as a Fuel." For the record, I would like to submit chapter 9, entitled "Hydrogen R. & D. Evaluations," chapter 10 of that report, which deals with the international hydrogen programs, and chapter 11, with their findings and recommendations.

I would also like to suggest that you have members of your staff review the entire report. Let me say here, parenthetically—I have only two paragraphs left—that I want to suggest that not all of these reports include just positive aspects of hydrogen research. At this point of our consideration, we have to realize that there are negatives that our research will have to overcome. I would also like to mention that in November 1979, I was invited to the proceedings of the Department of Energy, Chemical Energy Storage and Hydrogen Energy Systems Contracts Review, sponsored by the DOE at the Sheraton International Conference Center in Reston, Va.

I can attest to the fact that from all the models on display and the people I talk with, there is more than a cursory interest in this viable energy alternative. In fact, as most of you on this committee are aware, this week thousands of experts in the field are meeting in Japan to discuss the future uses of hydrogen. My hope is that you would see fit to have another set of hearings shortly to permit many of those people, in Japan now, time to testify on a more scientific and, I am sure, more eloquent basis than I am able to do here today. To do less, I am afraid, would be a great injustice to your consideration of this hydrogen bill and the subject matter that you are discussing here today.

Let me conclude by saying that hydrogen is a renewable source of energy, is nonpolluting, and has the potential for being cost effective. Let us look further at the dream we have just embarked upon and see the air of Los Angeles, New York, Washington, and other cities free from smog and pollution caused by auto exhaust, or the asthmatic who can breathe better and have his hospital costs and confinements reduced as a result of hospitalization from respiratory illness. No more out-of-gas lines and the robbing of people's income by OPEC countries would be another result of increased use of hydrogen. Well, this can go on and on with no end in sight.

Today we have the potential to take that dream and make it a reality or to turn it into a nightmare, and the choice belongs to each of us in this Congress of the United States as we consider these alternatives.

Thank you very much.

[The prepared statement of Mr. Grassley follows:]

CONGRESSMAN CHARLES E. GRASSLEY
Testimony Before
Subcommittee on Energy Development and Applications
Subcommittee on Energy Research and Production
"HYDROGEN"

Mr. Chairman:

It is a pleasure for me to be able to discuss the topic of "Hydrogen"
with you and members of your respective subcommittees today.

I would like to preface my remarks by saying to each of you I am deeply
appreciative to each of you for this opportunity to speak and offer you my
sincere congratulations for the wisdom you exemplify here today in bringing
up this viable energy alternative. Today's hearings on hydrogen, I believe,
will be the beginning of a new frontier for this country and the world and
will be the first step in turning the dreams of all mankind into the reality
of energy independence.

Let us all hope that as we embark upon the road of energy independence
that we let our minds daydream for a moment by the roadside. For like the
story of the tortoise and the hare, victory does not always come to the swift
But let us instead provide all mankind with the knowledge and assurance that
we will explore energy alternatives in all of its forms, at a price which is
reasonable and fair, is renewable in nature to the greatest extent possible
and is free as can humanly be expected from harming our environment, not
only for this generation, but for generations to come.

As supplies of crude oil diminish and prices get higher we must begin
to question ourselves as to whether this government is doing the most that
it can to find another source of fuel to heat our homes and fuel our
vehicles. More importantly we should be asking ourselves, is there any
renewable source of energy right here in this country that might help stop
the hemorrhage of dollars to the OPEC nations? I respectfully submit to
you that I believe the answer to this question is an emphatic, yes!

We have the power to tap coal, shale, tar sands, nuclear power, solar power, and various agricultural products for making gasohol, methanol and ethanol to generate electricity and produce vehicular fuel. However, as important and maybe more important is the topic we are here to discuss today, Hydrogen.

On September 25, 1979 I introduced the first comprehensive piece of legislation ever introduced in this Congress, H. R. 5399, which provides for the research, development and production and use of hydrogen as an alternative fuel. H. R. 5399 also amends the Internal Revenue Code of 1954, to encourage the production and the use of hydrogen as a fuel. The bill provide for tax incentives for hydrogen production and for certain equipment which uses hydrogen. Residential and business credits similar to the Code for Solar and Wind are provided for in the bill. Title I-Section 104 of the bill provides for Guaranteed Loans (not to exceed 90% of the aggregate cost with full payment not to exceed 20 years), Price or Purchase Guarantees and such other assistance of the Secretary is otherwise authorized by law to provide.

My bill specifically addresses the production of hydrogen by (1) Coal gasification (including high sulfur content) lignite, peat, char or residual oils (2) Ocean Thermal Energy Conversion (3) Electrolytic means (4) Low-head hydroelectric, (5) Solar, and (6) other means as the secretary deems necessary. I fully realize that there may be other means available such as fusion, which I also believe this Committee and the Secretary should be encouraged to pursue.

Some of the potential uses of hydrogen that I see for the future are:

1. Mixture of Hydrogen with natural gas (it is my understanding that we can presently add up to 15% hydrogen into existing natural gas pipelines with no adverse effect.

2. Fuel for rail and air transportation. Special application such as fuel lift trucks, mining and agricultural equipment busses, fleet vehicles and other multi-passenger vehicles designed for short distance travel.

3. Hydrogen fuel cells for power generation.

4. Hydrogen used to produce ammonia rather than natural gas to be used in making chemical fertilizer.

In other words hydrogen could be used to heat and cool our homes, cook our meals and provide a fuel to power almost every type of mode of vehicular transportation. It could reduce the consumption of natural gas, which is a non-renewable source of energy. Thereby making sure we have sufficient quantities of energy for or petrochemical industries and industries for making agricultural fertilizer as well as all other types of industries which rely on natural gas.

Mr. Chairman, I have worked with many people in the scientific, educational, industrial and governmental community in drafting H. R. 5399. My conversations with them lead me to believe that the potential realization of this alternative energy source is far from being realized. In Provo, Utah, it is my understanding that a complete hydrogen homestead is in operation. I have seen for myself a Dodge Omni powered by hydrogen and that a bus is running in Riverside, California on this fuel. It is also my understanding that one of our major aircraft manufacturers is in the planning stages of building a supersonic aircraft to fly on hydrogen. We have been in contact with people like the Billings Energy Corporation, General Electric, Teledyne Corporation, John Hopkins University, Jet Propulsion Laboratory, Westinghouse, Air Products and Chemical Inc., Rockwell, Monanto, United Technology, Marion Works, Consumer Solar Electric, and many others who are presently doing work in this field already, or are presently contemplating doing more if we take the lead. It has also been brought to my attention that several oil companies are also doing some research into this field, since apparently they feel an eventual need for alternative energies must be found.

The unfortunate part in all of this is that the Administration has not seen fit to place a stronger emphasis into the field of Research and Development of hydrogen. In fact, we have seen a steady decrease in their level of funding. The only encouraging part in all of this is that I had sent letters to all the Conferees of the Syn-fuel Bill asking them to include hydrogen into the terminology of a Synthetic-fuel. As you are aware, the conferees in their wisdom, did include hydrogen in the bill. As a result we must use this first step as a pivotal point since hydrogen was only included to a limited degree.

Recently the National Research Council issued a report on "Hydrogen as a fuel". For the record I would like to submit Chapter IX, Hydrogen R & D evaluation, Chapter X of that report which deals with International Hydrogen Programs, and Chapter XI, their findings and recommendations. I would also like to suggest that you have members of your staff review the entire report.

I would also like to mention that in November, 1979, I was invited to the proceedings of the D.O.E. Chemical Energy Storage and Hydrogen Energy Systems Contracts Review, sponsored by D.O.E. at the Sheraton International Conference Center in Reston, Virginia. I can attest to the fact that from the models on display and the people I talked with, that there is more than a cursory interest in this viable energy alternative. In fact, as most of you are aware, this week thousands of experts in the field are meeting in Japan to discuss the future uses of Hydrogen. It would be my hope that you would see fit to have another set of hearings shortly to permit many of the people time to testify on a more scientific and I'm sure, more elegant basis than I am today. To do less I am afraid, would be a great injustice to the American people.

Let me conclude by saying that hydrogen is a renewable source of energy,
is non-polluting and has the potential for being cost-effective. Let us look
further at the dream we have just embarked upon and see the air of Los Angeles
New York, Washington and other cities, free from the smog and pollution caused
by auto exhausts; or the asthmatic who can breath better, hospital costs and
confinements being reduced due to respiratory ailments. No more out of gas
lines or the robbing of peoples incomes by foreign countries. The list can
go on and on with no end in sight. Today we have the potential to take that
dream and make it a reality or turn it into a nightmare. The choice belongs
to each of us and how we will be perceived by generations for years to come
is ours alone. Pleasant dreams.

CHAPTER IX

HYDROGEN R&D EVALUATION

Whether, when, and to what extent hydrogen may be regarded as a likely
contender in the energy arena will depend on a web of factors--technical,
economic, environmental, legal, and institutional. Therefore, a realistic assessment of hydrogen calls for analysis of the full range of
benefits and costs associated with its generation, transmission, storage,
and end use. The assessment process will be far from simple, however,
in that some of the environmental concerns mitigated by hydrogen's clean
burning and non-polluting properties will be exacerbated by probable
sources and methods for its expanded generation. Moreover, the extended
time periods over which uncertain cost estimates must be projected make
economic comparisons difficult. To rate tomorrow's potential fuel by
yesterday's market values could prejudice the case against research into
and development of new energy options, possibly at the very moment in
history when international politics and policy must play a more important role in decisions about energy than today's cost accounting estimates.
       Hydrogen's advantages are conventionally identified as its
abundance, its clean burning, its high energy content, and the fact
that it can be recycled. It is capable of serving all energy sectors--
commercial, residential, and industrial--and can be used in automobiles,
aircraft, and rocket engines as well as for a heating fuel. A drawback,
according to present reckoning, is that by today's comparative standards
it is expensive. A synthetic fuel, it is a carrier and not a source of
energy. The fact that it must be produced from hydrocarbons or from
water means that various categories of costs must enter into the picture,
specifically the environmental, economic, and social costs associated
with the energy resources from which the hydrogen would be derived.
Elusive, but just as important, are the opportunity costs that must be
taken seriously in an era when upheavals of the international political
scene that are associated with the production and consumption of energy
from many of the present hydrocarbon sources have profound effects on
the total energy picture.
       Whether, when, and to what extent hydrogen will seem to be a de-
sirable fuel may depend on factors outside the technical state-of-the-art
and more on the state of the world. Nonetheless, the technical know-how
is a _sine qua non_; hydrogen cannot be regarded as a logical option unless the technical particulars of its generation, transmission, and
storage are explored to their full potential.

. Customary cost/benefit analyses make it clear that hydrogen's benign end-use properties will be partially offset by the deleterious effects of its production. When coal sources are considered, air quality land use, consumption of other resources (especially water), and disposal of wastes have all been identified as problems that could adversely affect hydrogen's desirability[1]. Even hydrogen production from water would not be an unmixed blessing because of the myriad of concerns with both nuclear and coal-fired electrical power plants. A recent workshop, jointly sponsored by the National Bureau of Standards, the Department of Energy, the National Science Foundation, the Electric Power Research Institute, the National Oceanic and Atmospheric Administration, and the Committee on Science and Technology of the U.S. House of Representatives, specifically recommended that a proper assessment of hydrogen as a fuel should move beyond the usual questions based on a limited view of economics and technology[2]. A detailed comparison of hydrogen with other fuels taking into full account all of the social and environmental ramifications should be performed. An important question that would emerge would be whether the reduction in external impacts at the point of use would be sufficient to outweigh the costs associated with production. Such a focus might be useful in setting R&D policy by identifying problem areas where a breakthrough in technology at some crucial stage might alter advantageously the balance between costs and benefits.

Even with the sources of hydrogen remaining virtually unchanged, certain environmental considerations may tip the balance in its favor. Assuming that coal becomes a major source of hydrogen in the future, even such environmental problems as land disturbance, water use, and air pollution associated with hydrogen production might be less harmful than the direct burning of coal. If coal must be used to meet our near-term energy needs, conversion to hydrogen may be attractive, both economically and environmentally, based on air quality considerations.

According to a study conducted by the National Academy of Sciences[3] the continuing increase of carbon dioxide in the atmosphere is a matter of great concern. While there is no agreement on the exact nature of or the timetable for climatic effects of CO_2 release, the consequences may be dire. The report concludes, "The prospect of damaging climatic changes may thus be a stimulus for greater efforts at conservation and a more rapid transition to alternate energy sources than is justified by economic considerations alone."

The narrow application of conventional "engineering economics" in technology assessments of hydrogen fuel futures may form too limited a framework for valid energy R&D decisions to be made. In fact, the cost/benefit analysis performed prematurely can become a deadening guideline in the design of R&D programs. Many of the benefits may be long in coming; many of the values may elude quantification. Under such circumstances, preoccupation with economic considerations may divert attention from the wider set of societal issues that only come into focus if we view the future with a premise that hydrogen may become a feasible energy option.

Judicious restriction of the cost/benefit analysis to the resolu-
tion of near term development and demonstration decisions is indicated.
Such major, near-term funding decisions should bear the scrutiny of
economic analyses; the longer term, more basic research opportunities
should not.

In the consideration of appropriate R&D to establish the role and
place for hydrogen in the energy equation, it will be important that
its safety aspects be thoroughly explored and understood before decisions are attempted regarding its deployment as a consumer fuel. The
hazards associated with its use must be carefully assessed for each
potential application, for although hydrogen may be safer than gasoline
or methane for some applications, it may be more hazardous in others.
Actually, a great amount of technical information on hydrogen safety
properties is already in hand[4], but there will be a tendency to attack
hydrogen as a highly flammable and explosive fuel because it is a new
and unfamiliar fuel. Such criticism must be anticipated at a time
when the public is increasingly insistent that it be allowed to participate in making technical decisions affecting its future. It will be
imperative, therefore, that gaps in information about the safety of
hydrogen be filled before the public is asked to accept a new fuel form

CHAPTER X

INTERNATIONAL HYDROGEN PROGRAMS

Present efforts on hydrogen programs in some countries of Western Europe
are greater than in the United States. These programs encompass work on
hydrogen production by electrochemical and thermochemical means, use in
transportation vehicles, and as supporting work on pipeline transmission
and distribution. Projects are generally a mix of long-term and near-
term technologies for applications which are self-evident to countries
which have a few or no native energy resources, but are totally dependent
on imported energy. Some European countries and Japan have no significant
fossil fuel resources, i.e., oil, natural gas or coal. Their interest
in alternative fuels which can be derived from abundant, e.g., nuclear
or renewable non-fossil resources, is imperative for their ultimate survival. Countries like Brazil and our neighbors in Canada, who have
abundant hydroelectric resources, are well aware that hydrogen production from such resources is an attractive option. In Germany, work is
in progress on advanced high temperature nuclear reactors which have
the potential to be the source of energy to produce hydrogen by electrolytic means coupled with high efficiency electric conversion devices, or
with direct heat using thermochemical production processes. The Japanese
see a logical connection between solar energy and hydrogen production
processes.

It is of value to mention some special accomplishments in the area of
hydrogen made abroad in various countries.

In the Netherlands, pioneering work was done on metal hydrides of the
rare earths such as $LaNi_5$. A systems study was done which showed that
combined electric and hydrogen systems may be optimal in the Netherlands.
Presently, there are no intensive R&D programs on hydrogen, but they are
a participant in the International Energy Agency (IEA) effort in electrolytic hydrogen production, i.e., Annex IV and V.

The European Community, which consists of a collection of western
European countries who contribute to the R&D budget, supports major programs on hydrogen at the Joint Research Centre (JRC) at Ispra. In addition, major contractual efforts in hydrogen are in progress with industrial firms. The JRC has the largest effort in the world on thermochemical hydrogen production. An important piece of work has been a
major marketing study on future uses of hydrogen. They have recently
demonstrated a bench-scale hybrid electro-chemical-thermochemical hydrogen production process, i.e., Mark-13.

West Germany has similar interest in hydrogen production and does work on thermochemical processes that can be driven by high temperature nuclear heat sources under development. The leading manufacturer of advanced electrolyzers is Lurgi Company, which is located in West Germany. The Daimler-Benz Company of West Germany has major work in progress on hydrogen-fueled vehicles. Their most significant accomplishment is the design and operation of vehicles operating on dual hydride bed of iron titanium and magnesium-nickel alloys originally developed in the U.S. Presently, discussions regarding possible programs in this area have been begun between U.S. DOE and the German Federal Ministry for Research and Technology. In these discussions, they have indicated that a 30 man-year effort is in progress in Germany.

Both Italy and Switzerland have work in progress on advanced alka-line electrolyzers. The De Nora Corporation and Brown Boveri of Italy and Switzerland, respectively, have built some of the largest industrial electrolysis plants and are each supporting in-house R&D efforts, as well as working on contracts from their respective governments.

In Japan, the "Sunshine Project" is a broad-base hydrogen research program. Emphasis is on solar-assisted hydrogen production. They have done pioneer work on direct electrolytic production from sunlight with semi-conductors which has stimulated similar work in the U.S.

Advanced electrolyzer development is under way in Canada in a joint effort between Electrolyzer Corporation of America, Noranda Corporation and the Canadian Government. Large undeveloped hydroelectric resources exist in Canada which could be developed quickly in the medium term. There is good reason to believe that a portion of this renewable resource could be sold to the U.S. Evidence for hydrogen markets in the U.S. could encourage development of these hydroelectric resources in Canada.

In Brazil, with its vast remote hydroelectric resources in the Amazon, there are programs in progress to develop electrolyzer technology and ultimately an electrolytic equipment industry. The Gas Company of Rio, which today delivers a 50-50 vol. % mixture of hydrogen and carbon monoxide (H_2-CO) has interest in adding electrolytic hydrogen to their city gas distribution system. They presently produce the H_2-CO mixture by reforming naptha imported from the Middle East. Discussion between U.S. DOE and the Brazilian Government on possible cooperative programs was initiated, but further discussions have been delayed pending resolu-tion of unrelated issues.

Some of the work mentioned above is covered under existing or pending IEA agreements on hydrogen production, i.e., Annexes I, II, and IV and V, respectively. The Annexes deal with thermochemical hydrogen production (I and II), assessment (III), and electrolyte production (IV and V). The participants in these Annexes are:

o Belgium
o Canada
o European Economic Community
o Germany
o Italy
o Japan
o Netherlands
o Sweden
o Switzerland
o United Kingdom
o United States

The IEA cooperative activities are either in progress or about to be finalized. Formal exchange of information on Annexes I, II and III has begun. Copies of these Annexes are available from DOE.

The French, although not a participant in the IEA effort, have a major program in place on development of advanced electrolytic hydrogen production processes (Electricite De France). They foresee important industrial uses of hydrogen in the near term, and eventually a hydrogen pipeline grid in France. Gas De France has completed a preliminary study of the feasibility of underground storage of hydrogen and found no major technical obstacles. They have expressed an interest in possible exchange of information with similar DOE programs.

SUMMARY

1.   Various cooperative efforts are in progress or pending between U.S., European countries and the Japanese on hydrogen production.
2.   The level of effort in hydrogen R&D in western Europe is significantly greater than in the U.S.
3.   Possible cooperative efforts on hydrogen-fueled vehicles are under discussions with the Germans.
4.   Discussions with Brazil regarding possible cooperative efforts were begun but are delayed for unrelated reasons.
5.   Cooperative programs with the Canadians in the area of hydrogen production are logical because of the close proximity of the source (Canadian hydroelectric) and markets (U.S.) as well as good political relations between the two countries.
6.   Informal inquiries have been made by BNL to the French on possible interest in exchange of information with the U.S. on DOE programs dealing with underground storage of hydrogen.

16

CHAPTER XI

FINDINGS AND RECOMMENDATIONS

Hydrogen is currently important in the U.S. economy as a major chemical
intermediate, as a reducing gas, and for a variety of special applications. It has a potential as a fuel for such applications as automobiles
and aircraft, where its cleanliness and high energy content offer operating advantages, and may ultimately serve as a replacement for natural gas
o r petroleum by delivering and storing energy derived from non-fossil
(nuclear and solar) sources. In this latter case hydrogen would be considered as a carrier of energy, analogous to electricity, rather than as
a primary energy source.

Current annual consumption of the order of 3 trillion standard
cubic feet corresponds to an energy content of about 1 quad (10^{15}Btu).
Most is produced and consumed onsite as a feedstock commodity by the
chemical and petroleum refining industries that comprise about 95 percent of the present market. Most of the remaining "merchant" hydrogen
is also used for feedstock purposes. Little is consumed as a fuel.
High performance space rockets constitute the principal current fuel
users, although industrial waste gases containing hydrogen are occasionally blended with natural gas for heating purposes, and there are a number of locations where pure hydrogen, produced as a byproduct, is burned
on its own for industrial heating applications.

As long as fossil fuel sources continue to remain available and
useable at reasonable costs, natural or synthetic hydrocarbons will
probably continue to compete with electricity as the preferred energy
carriers of the future. If, however, either fuel depletions or environmental restrictions limit the future economical availability of conventional fossil fuel sources, it will become necessary to shift fuel dependence in part or wholly from fossil to non-fossil sources. When, for
example, oil and gas supplies become limited, there will be an impetus
to expand nuclear and solar energy resources and to accelerate the manufacture of synthetic fuels, including hydrogen, from coal.

Although the U.S. is fortunate in having enough coal reserves to
last a very long time, even at accelerated rates of consumption, it cannot be assumed that unlimited supplies of coal will be available in the
future. It may not prove possible to markedly expand coal production
rates because of labor shortages or environmental restriction on extraction, processing, or shipment. Other environmental restrictions at the
point of use may make the consumption of coal increasingly expensive.

Finally, a possibility exists that carbon combustion may be curtailed in the future in order to control increases in atmospheric CO_2 content.

If it becomes necessary to limit coal consumption, the alternate energy sources would appear to be either nuclear (fission and/or fusion) or solar, which, generally speaking, yield either heat or electricity as their primary outputs. Cost effective means do not exist for the long-distance transmission of heat per se. Therefore such energy sources would have to be converted to electricity or to some other form of energy carrier, such as hydrogen, to make them widely useful. Several reasons suggest that hydrogen might be competitive to electricity as an energy carrier in spite of its higher production cost:

o The costs and environmental impacts of hydrogen transmission and distribution are more favorable than those for electricity.
o Some end uses lend themselves to hydrogen use. For example, it should be more economic to convert existing oil and gas burning equipment to use hydrogen than to replace it with equivalent electrical equipment,
o It should be simpler and cheaper to store hydrogen than to store electricity.

An improved understanding of coal use problems in general, and CO_2 problems in particular, including the dimensions of necessary solutions, may become clear within a decade. Because results may be negative in terms of expanded coal consumption, it would be prudent to have R&D results in hand by that time that would enable early implementing decisions on alternate energy resources to be made, including those that would relate to the future role and extent of hydrogen as a fuel. This does not mean that hydrogen production capabilities need to be poised in useful form. The deployment of large amounts of non-fossil energy sources would take a number of years, during which the hydrogen production technologies could be refined and constructed. Thus, although basic and applied research on non-carbon hydrogen production techniques and technologies should be conducted within the next few years in order to provide a technical foundation for possible implementation, the more expensive development and demonstration activities can probably be deferred until the need for non-carbon-sourced hydrogen is more positively understood.

In contrast to the uncertainties about the future of hydrogen as a fuel, the present trend of steady increases in the use of feedstock hydrogen is expected to continue. By the year 2000, for example, estimates of such consumption range up to three times current levels for the industrial areas now using hydrogen. New requirements for ore reduction and for the refining of shale oil and synthetic fuels from coal could add further additional hydrogen markets if these processes become widely used. These added feedstock requirements will probably either be met by expanded methane reforming -- only about 3% of the total U.S. annual natural gas consumption is currently used for such purposes -- or, as economic or political factors dictate, by coal conversion processes.

It is fairly certain that a widespread market for hydrogen as a fuel will not materialize until it is forced by hydrocarbon limitations. Prospects for the near-term adoption of hydrogen as a fuel are considered to be low. For example, there is no economic reason to contemplate the conversion of natural gas to hydrogen in order to serve as an alternate gaseous heating fuel. On the other hand, while there are some urban air pollution imporvements that could accrue if hydrogen were used as a propulsive fuel in place of liquid hydrocarbons, it is questionable that large amounts of natural gas would be diverted from gaseous heating and feedstock roles to manufacture hydrogen for use as a transportation fuel. Thus, if a fuel market for hydrogen is developed, it is probable that the fuel would have to come either from non-carbon sources or as an end product of a coal/synthetic-fuel chain. Neither route is economically attractive for the near term in comparison with competitive fuels from the same raw materials.

Electrolysis is very capital intensive because of the large required investments for electricity generation. Similarly, although hard designs of thermochemical systems for decomposing water are not available, analyses of preliminary concepts indicate large capital investments may be necessary. Thus, although the feedstock (water) costs are virtually nil, the end product cost of non-carbon hydrogen is high.

Unfavorable economics are also encountered in the derivation of hydrogen from coal. In comparison with the manufacture of synthetic natural gas (SNG), hydrogen extraction from coal requires a greater capital investment and more energy. As a result, gaseous hydrogen can be expected to cost 20 to 50% more than SNG, per Btu. Synthetic coal liquids, which are more expensive than SNG, could approximate gaseous hydrogen in cost; however, since both the fuel distribution infrastructure for transportation fuels and the ultimate user vehicles are geared to liquid hydrocarbons, overall transportation system cost advantages would be expected to remain with the synthetic liquid fuels. Any reduction in the future costs of producing hydrogen will also reduce the cost of synthetic liquid fuels, since much of the latter's cost derives from its hydrogen enrichment. Thus, relative cost ratios of coal-sourced hydrogen and coal liquids should not be expected to change appreciably in the future.

Generally speaking, cost considerations will inhibit the use of hydrogen as a transportation fuel unless the environmental penalties of using synthetic gasoline or diesel fuels prove to be high. In the case of automobiles, potential hydrogen applications will be competing with synthetic fuels in the near-term and advanced storage battery electric cars in the longer term. The development of a low cost, highly efficient hydrogen/air fuel cell might capture automotive markets for hydrogen in the competition with advanced batteries, since there are not the same fundamental, basic chemical limitations to fuel cell performance that there are to batteries--but hydrogen/air fuel cells are not receiving current R&D attention.

Civil transport aircraft of the future may also create a market for hydrogen as a transportation fuel. Because of its high energy density, a liquid-hydrogen fueled supersonic aircraft would be able to operate at ranges in excess of those possible with hydrocarbon fuels, and thus make non-stop trans-Pacific type flights practical. If a national goal for the development of a long-range supersonic transport were to be adopted, serious consideration should be given to the use of hydrogen as a fuel.

In spite of reservations about the timing and rate of impact of hydrogen as a fuel, there is a need for a well conceived R&D program to study some of the basic problems that constrain its entrance into the economy. Specifically, the following principles should guide the formulation of a U.S. program in support of hydrogen systems:

o Basic exploratory research should be pursued on innovative concepts for hydrogen production, transmission, storage, and utilization through the laboratory demonstration stages. Such research should be pursued even if near-term market needs cannot be identified.

o The federal program should include R&D elements designed to create a national data base of sufficient depth and quality that sound evaluations can be made of program alternatives in the future selection of coherent and timely development and demonstration programs.

o The federal program should defer large-scale system development and demonstration activities aimed at hydrogen production until a market need of significant magnitude is clearly identified and it is established that the timing or risks make it unlikely that the private sector will undertake these R&D phases.

o The architects of hydrogen R&D programs should remain alert to developments in applications areas that might enhance the need for hydrogen, and thus accelerate consideration of development and demonstration programs for production, transmission, and storage systems.

o Program priority should be given to exploratory research on concepts that hold promise of signifcantly reducing hydrogen production costs, particularly for coal/hydrogen systems where the cost reductions could also benefit synthetic fuel costs.

o Research should be initiated on hydrogen/air fuel-cells suitable for transportation applications to provide an alternative to battery powered automobiles in the event that future hydrocarbon fuel limitations are encountered.

o In addition to work on hydrogen production concepts, appropriate R&D should also be conducted on potential problems associated with the transmission and storage of hydrogen as a consumer fuel. Particular attention should be given to the identification and resolution of potential safety problems for all phases of the hydrogen chain from

production to consumption. Such studies should be
conducted in a timely fashion so as to contribute to
the overall evaluation of the feasibility of proposed
hydrogen systems.

In constructing an appropriate R&D program, it must be recognized
that other nations are also engaged in hydrogen research based upon their
perceived possible future needs for non-carbon-sourced hydrogen. These
needs may be both earlier and greater than those of the U.S., depending
upon each nation's lifestyle and access to natural gas and coal. The
present U.S. program accepts the probability that these foreign needs
may bring a likelihood of foreign technology leadership, and does not
attempt to fully duplicate foreign research efforts. This should continue as the basic U.S. position; however, the U.S. should maintain an
R&D program that is sufficiently advanced to enable it to participate
in meaningful international technology exchange programs. The research
areas in the U.S. program should, however, be those that are clearly
applicable to its domestic interests and energy outlook.

Mr. OTTINGER. Thank you very much. I share your enthusiasm for hydrogen as a fuel and hope we will get some encouragement from our experts today in being able to produce that economically.

Mr. Davis, do you have any questions?

Mr. DAVIS. Thank you, Mr. Chairman. I just want to congratulate Congressman Grassley for his interest in this subject. I know we are not holding a hearing on any particular bill, but I just wonder, Congressman Grassley, if the bill you introduced, H.R. 5399, has a cost factor in it.

Mr. GRASSLEY. We specifically did not do that because of the very limited research done on that point, and rather than put a figure in that so often is greatly underestimated or maybe even have it be too high, because of not having the research done on it, I left that out. I would like to have this committee take those points of view into consideration when you have gotten your hearings done and put all this together and come up with a figure that is reasonable. I do want to suggest to you, though, that with the inclusion of this subject matter in the synfuels conference report, specific reference given to hydrogen research that funds available there within the limits and considering the priorities that will have to be given to the synthetic fuel expenditure, there is a great potential there for money going into this within the limits of the other priorities set by that legislation.

Mr. DAVIS. I'm sure the chairman of this subcommittee, Mr. Ottinger, who has been a diligent person in looking for alternative sources of fuel, will become heavily involved in that, and I thank the gentleman for his testimony.

Mr. OTTINGER. We thank you very much. We will certainly consider the legislation that you have introduced.

We now have a panel of witnesses—if you would all come forward at this point. It consists of Dr. Frank O'Brien, general manager, direct energy conversion programs, General Electric Co., Wilmington, Mass.; Dr. James E. Funk, associate vice president of academic affairs, University of Kentucky, Lexington, Ky.; Dr. Hilde Lindsey, program manager, solar hydrogen production program, Solar Energy Research Institute, Golden, Colo., who is accompanied by Dr. Arthur Nozik, branch chief of the photoconversion branch. If you would come to the witness table.

Without objection, the full statements of all the witnesses will appear in the record, including Congressman Grassley's statement.

We would welcome it if you could summarize your statements. If you want to read them though, you are welcome to do so. Why don't we start with Dr. Funk.

STATEMENT OF DR. JAMES E. FUNK

Dr. FUNK. Thank you, Mr. Chairman.

I appreciate the opportunity to appear before this committee to discuss the thermochemical production of hydrogen from water. I do have a brief statement highlighting my views of the important aspects of this question, and I would be pleased to attempt to answer questions after the statement.

For more detailed information, I would like to refer you to a recent review article prepared by Dr. Kennedy E. Cox of the Los Alamos

Scientific Laboratory. A full reference to that review article is included in my statement.

Hydrogen can be produced from water in one of three ways. The first and most commonly practiced procedure today is by a reaction of water with some carbon-containing material such as natural gas. The majority of hydrogen produced in the world today comes from reacting water with natural gas.

The second technique is water electrolysis, a procedure known since 1800, in which an electric current is passed through a conducting solution containing water, producing hydrogen and oxygen.

The third technique is by means of a series of chemical reactions which in sum result only in the consumption of water and the production of hydrogen and oxygen. Thermochemical hydrogen production, about which I've been asked to speak, is in this third category.

Carbonaceous sources, such as oil and gas, are scarce and expensive and will be even more so in the future. Water electrolysis is expensive because all the energy processed has to be supplied by electricity. Thermochemical processes offer the potential for higher efficiency and lower cost because the energy required by the process can be supplied as heat rather than electricity. The cost involved in the conversion to electricity is thereby avoided.

A large number of possible thermochemical cycles have appeared in the literature in the past 7 to 8 years. Many of these should not really be called processes, however, since they are usually simply a set of chemical reactions which sum up to water decomposition. Reactions in the cycles are normally chosen because they have certain thermodynamic characteristics which suggest the potential for high efficiency and/or because they are known reactions. A great deal of work needs to be done before any cycle or set of reactions can really be called a process. That brings me to the five major points I want to make today.

The first of these points is that the development of the science and technology of thermochemical processes is just beginning. It is only since 1972 to 1974 that more than one small group of people have paid serious attention to this technology.

The first work done in the United States on thermochemical processes was done in the early 1960's at General Motors. It is being vigorously pursued in the United States at this time by only Westinghouse, the General Atomic Co., and the Institute of Gas Atomic Co., and the Institute of Gas Technology.

The second point is, the thermochemical decomposition of water is prototypical of processes which produce a synthetic fuel from a renewable source and high temperature heat. I think that's an important point to emphasize, and let me say it again: These are processes which take water and heat and produce hydrogen, which is a fuel. A number of these kinds of processes are possible. They are going to be very important in the future. The problem of producing a truly synthetic fuel from a renewable source of heat will be very important in the future, and thermochemical decomposition of water is prototypical of those processes.

The third point is that both basic and applied research are required for the proper development of this technology. Basic information on the chemistry of the reactions and on materials is required in order to do the process design and prepare flow sheets. There is no way to tell what the actual efficiency or cost will be without doing this sort of work.

The fourth point is that the high temperature heat source which provides the heat for thermochemical processes may be nuclear fission or fusion or solar. Additional work is required on the heat source itself, as well as on the high temperature heat exchangers which are required to move heat into the process.

The fifth and last point is that very little work has been done in the United States on the cost of thermochemical processes. Our efforts have been directed mainly toward basic chemistry studies and materials studies. Preliminary engineering designs and cost estimates need to be made for the processes being developed by Westinghouse and General Atomic.

The capital cost for thermochemical plants—very rough and very preliminary—in 1979 dollars, ranges from $600 to $1,000 per kilowatt of hydrogen, a factor of almost two. The overall process efficiency varies from 35 to 55 percent. The softness and the range of these numbers reflects the fact that development of this technology is in a very early stage.

That concludes my statement, Mr. Chairman. I'll be pleased to attempt to answer questions now.

[The prepared statement of Dr. Funk follows:]

HYDROGEN PRODUCTION BY THE THERMOCHEMICAL

DECOMPOSITION OF WATER*

James E. Funk

Associate Vice President for Academic Affairs
Coordinator of Energy Research
Director, Institute for Mining and Minerals Research

University of Kentucky
Lexington, Kentucky 40506

I appreciate the opportunity to appear before this
committee to discuss the thermochemical production of hydrogen
from water. I intend to make a brief statement highlighting my
view of the important points relating to the development of
thermochemical processes and will be pleased to attempt to answer
questions. For more detailed information, I refer you to a
recent review prepared by Dr. Kenneth E. Cox of the Los Alamos
Scientific Laboratory.[†]

Hydrogen can be produced from water in one of three
ways:

    1)   a chemical reaction with a material containing

        carbon, such as natural gas

    2)   by water electrolysis

---

*Presented at a joint hearing of the Subcommittee on
Energy Research and Production and the Subcommittee on Energy
Development and Applications (House Committee on Science and
Technology) Washington D. C., June 25, 1980.

[†]"Thermochemical Production of Hydrogen from Water: A
Critical Review" by Dr. Kenneth E. Cox, Chapter 9 of "Production
of Synthetic Gas from Nuclear Energy Sources," LA-7592-MS, U. S.
Government Printing Office: 1979-677-013/58, prepared by Los
Alamos Scientific Laboratory for the Texas Gas Transmission
Corporation under contract no. EW-78-Y-04-4183 with the U. S.
Department of Energy, April, 1979.

3) a series of chemical reactions which in sum
    result only in the consumption of water and
    the generation of hydrogen and oxygen.

Carbonaceous sources such as oil and gas are and will
be in short supply and expensive. Water electrolysis is
expensive because all the energy consumed by the process is
supplied as electricity. Thermochemical processes offer the
potential for higher efficiency and lower cost because the energy
required to decompose water is supplied as heat rather than
electricity or some other more expensive form of energy. When a
thermochemical process is actually built it will closely resemble
a chemical plant in that there will be chemical reaction vessels,
separators, distillation columns and other process equipment. In
addition, there will be a great deal of heat exchange since high
efficiency demands a minimum of heat rejection from the process.
In the course of accomplishing the chemical reactions which
comprise the process it will be necessary to separate and recycle
any unreacted materials as well as to recover all available and
usable heat.

A large number of possible thermochemical cycles have
appeared in the literature in the past seven to eight years.
They should not be called "processes" since usually they are
simply a set of chemical reactions which add up to the
decomposition of water. The chemical reactions and the cycles
are normally chosen because they possess certain thermodynamic
properties which suggest the potential for high efficiency,
and/or because it is known that the chemical reactions actually
take place as they are written. A great deal of work must be

done before a cycle, or set of chemical reactions, becomes a
process, and that brings me to the major points I wish to make
today.

1) The development of the science and technology of
    thermochemical processes is just beginning. It
    is only since 1972-74 that more than one small
    group of people has paid serious attention to the
    question. The first work in the U.S. was done at
    the Allison Division of General Motors in the
    early 1960's. It is being vigorously pursued in
    the U. S. at this time only by Westinghouse and
    the General Atomic Company.

2) Thermochemical decomposition of water is
    protypical of processes which produce a synthetic
    fuel from a renewable source and high temperature
    heat. Such processes will surely be important in
    the future and it is necessary to understand the
    scientific, technological and economic aspects of
    the processes in detail.

3) Both basic and applied research are required for
    the proper development of this technology. Basic
    information on the chemistry of the reactions and
    on materials is required in order to prepare
    flowsheets and mass and energy balances which
    describe how the process would actually be built
    and operated. The process capital cost and
    overall thermal efficiency can then be
    determined. Both of these quantities determine

the cost to produce hydrogen.

4) The high temperature heat source which provides the heat for thermochemical processes may be nuclear fission or fusion, or solar. Additional work is required on the heat source itself as well as on the high temperature heat exchangers (both design and materials) which must move the heat into the process.

5) Very little work on the cost of thermochemical processes has been done in the U. S. Our effort has mainly been directed toward basic chemistry and materials. Preliminary engineering designs and cost estimates need to be made for the processes being developed by Westinghouse and General Atomic.

The capital cost for thermochemical plants, expressed in 1979 dollars and based upon earlier engineering designs and cost estimates which are both preliminary and very rough, are in the range 600 - 1100 $/kw hydrogen. The overall process thermal efficiency ranges from 35 to 55%. The current status of both cost and efficiency reflects the fact that the development of this technology is in the very early stages.

Mr. OTTINGER. Thank you very much, Dr. Funk.

I would like to interrupt our witnesses now because we have had join us the chairman of the Energy Research and Production Subcommittee of our Science and Technology Committee. He very much shares the interest I have in this subject. And his subcommittee is cosponsoring these hearings. We work very closely together on different aspects of solving our Nation's energy problems.

Congressman Mike McCormack from Washington.

Mr. McCORMACK. Thank you, Mr. Chairman.

I appreciate this opportunity to make an opening statement and I apologize for my tardiness.

These hearings can serve a great purpose for the Congress in establishing a basic understanding of this energy medium. The first thing, of course, is that hydrogen is not truly a source of energy, it must first be produced using some other primary source of energy. Ultimately this source of energy will probably be solar energy and nuclear energy via fission or fusion.

There is a great deal of potential for hydrogen as a fuel. Frankly, I anticipate toward the end of the century seeing hydrogen-fueled airplanes, at least experimental airplanes, flying in this country. I envision the time when we will have hydrogen production stations at such sites as, let us say, the airfield in Chicago, making hydrogen at the site and fueling the planes as they come and go. This is just one of many uses. I can see it ultimately replacing methane as a gaseous fuel. Of course, I see it as a fuel for ground vehicles.

There is a tremendous amount of work to be done. I think it is time that we get at it. We know enough about the technology to know that it can be very attractive. I think it is time for us to get going and I appreciate this opportunity to join with Congressman Ottinger in welcoming you all here today to these hearings which I think will initiate a positive program of action for bringing hydrogen into our list of practical fuels for this country. I thank you all for coming and I thank you, Mr. Chairman.

Mr. OTTINGER. I thank you for joining in these hearings. As we demonstrated yesterday, when McCormack and I get together anything can be done, like adding $107 million over the objection of the Appropriations Committee for solar and fusion and basic energy sciences.

Dr. O'Brien, we would like to hear from you next. We are pleased to have you with us.

STATEMENT OF DR. FRANK O'BRIEN

Dr. O'BRIEN. Thank you, Mr. Chairman and members of the subcommittee. I appreciate the opportunity to testify at this hearing today. It wasn't too many years ago that the quickest way to start a conversation or an argument was to bring up one of two subjects, either politics or religion. About the mid-1970's we added a third subject to this category, energy.

My testimony today is directed at one form of energy, hydrogen, its use, and its potential for a much larger role in future energy systems of this Nation and the world.

Hydrogen is valuable as a fuel and as a chemical feedstock. The generation of hydrogen is equivalent to the storage of energy in chemical form. Hydrogen fuel can be used ultimately to produce thermal energy from combustion and electrical energy from gas turbine generators and fuel cells.

The use of hydrogen as a feedstock for ammonia fertilizer production is growing rapidly. An increased production of ammonia can serve two purposes, to grow food not only for consumption in the United States but for the rapidly growing world population, and it can also serve as an energy carrier by transporting this ammonia through existing ammonia pipelines to geographically dispersed locations, decomposing the ammonia to use its hydrogen content in fuel cells and produce both central and dispersed electric power supplies.

The production of hydrogen by electric utilities can add to their operating flexibility. Hydrogen generated by water electrolysis during times of relatively low consumer demand for electricity can be reconverted to electricity in a fuel cell or gas turbine during peak load periods. It also can be transported by pipeline for reconversion to electricity near the end user. Hydrogen can also be used as an alternative fuel as a substitute for or supplement to natural gas, and, most important, is an environmentally clean fuel. In its combustion there is no release of carbon dioxide, and no contaminants such as sulfur species, which are released in the combustion of fossil fuels and result in the so-called acid rain experienced in many of our major industrial centers, are present in the combustion of hydrogen.

Perhaps on a much longer term, hydrogen could be a significant source of fuel in the transportation sector. As an example of its potential use in automotive engines, a major automobile manufacturer in Germany, Daimler-Benz, has been working since 1973 to adapt their standard automotive engines to burn pure hydrogen or a mixture of hydrogen and gasoline. In the near future they plan to demonstrate the practicality of the use of hydrogen as a substitute or supplemental automotive fuel by operating, initially, a fleet of 28 vehicles in the city of Berlin using town gas directly from the city's industrial and residential distribution network.

The basic technology for hydrogen distribution is well understood. Hydrogen can be transported in pipelines in substantially the same manner as natural gas. It can also be transported in various sizes of pressure vessels. During the heyday of the space programs in the 1960's and early 1970's very large million gallon types of liquid hydrogen storage facilities were constructed. In the United States, production and use of hydrogen has increased by a factor of 40 since 1945 and has tripled in the last decade. The energy resources used to produce this hydrogen are natural gas about 73 percent, petroleum 23 percent, and about 1 percent miscellaneous sources. It is ironic that the most environmentally clean method to produce hydrogen, water electrolysis, produces only a miniscule portion of this total production.

This Nation's annual requirement for hydrogen is anticipated to grow substantially from the present 1.4 quads of energy use to a minimum of 5.5 quads by the year 2000 and to as high as 22 quads, if hydrogen becomes a major factor in transportation fuel and the electric utility industry.

A cause for concern for hydrogen planners is that, in face of such a range of increased demand, the availability of natural gas and oil to produce this hydrogen may be decreasing. The obvious consequence, if unconventionual supplies of hydrogen are not developed in the interim period, is a serious shortfall of hydrogen to meet the increasing demand.

What would be the impact on the economy of this Nation if we suffered an energy shortfall in the future? If, for example, we suffered say a 15-percent total energy shortfall over the period 1978–1985, the average annual growth rate of our gross national product would fall a full point. The cumulative effect would be about $435 billion in current year dollars. This same 15-percent total energy shortfall would also mean a decline in the average annual growth rate of business investment to the tune of approximately $160 billion also in current year dollars. This would also mean approximately 3 million fewer jobs available at a time when it is estimated that over the next 10 years this Nation has to create at least 10 million new jobs for the unemployed and for new people entering the work force. This would be a particularly painful result of an energy shortfall. An example of this type of pain was experienced during the natural gas shortfall during the winter of 1976 and 1977. Approximately 1 million people were out of work for varying periods of time as a result of this, fortunately temporary, energy shortage.

In recognition of the need to develop methods to reduce the consumption of natural gas and oil, a major goal of the Department of Energy was established to develop technologies which permit substitution of renewable energy resources for natural gas and oil. This production of hydrogen from water using renewable energy resources such as solar, wind, hydroelectric, and ocean energy conversion systems, is one technology being pursued. Water electrolysis systems would provide an excellent option for converting geographically dispersed renewable resources to a storable and transportable energy form.

Interest in the development of renewable energy sources is growing. One example is a development sponsored by the DOE Office of Solar Technology for extracting useful energy from the solar heat stored in vast surface waters of the tropical and semitropical oceans. This ocean thermal energy system, OTEC, would utilize the temperature difference between warm surface and cold subsurface ocean waters to power turbines and produce electricity. For OTEC platforms located reasonably close to the land mass electrical energy could be cabled directly to shore. For those platforms located in ocean waters where it is impractical to directly transmit the electrical energy, an alternate energy carrier is required.

One of the most cost effective energy carriers which can be used in this type of application is ammonia produced from hydrogen generated by the electrolysis of water and combined with nitrogen from the air. This ammonia energy can then be readily transported to any geographic location. As an example of supplementing conventional energy, studies are being conducted by a major gas supplier to establish the feasibility of a large solar photovoltaic system to produce electrolytic hydrogen.

This hydrogen so produced would be used to supplement their natural gas supplies. Interest in renewable energy resources has also been expressed in Canada, Iceland, Greenland, Brazil, Africa, all of whom who have excess hydroelectric power and are facing the need for increased ammonia production for fertilizer and also the need for synthetic fuels.

If I may summarize, hydrogen has a great deal of flexibility as a future fuel and as an energy carrier and energy storage medium. It can be produced from water using power from renewable resources. It is an environmentally clean fuel, thereby contributing to a reduction in the growing air pollution many of our major cities are faced with today.

Hydrogen as a fuel will not only serve the growing energy needs of this nation, but is also capable of becoming an important factor in improving the U.S. balance of payments as an alternative to high cost imported oil and natural gas. The development of advanced technologies to produce and utilize hydrogen fuel, such as electrolyzers and fuel cells, is a critical element of this nation's drive toward future energy independence.

Thank you.

[The prepared statement of Dr. O'Brien follows:]

STATEMENT FOR

THE HOUSE SCIENCE & TECHNOLOGY COMMITTEE

SUBCOMMITTEE ON ENERGY RESEARCH & PRODUCTION

AND

SUBCOMMITTEE ON DEVELOPMENT & APPLICATION

ON

"HYDROGEN: PRODUCTION AND ENERGY USES"

By

Frank O'Brien
General Electric Company

Washington, D. C.

25 June 1980

Hydrogen, Its Use

and Future Potential as a Major Energy Form

It wasn't too many years ago that the quickest way to start a conversation, or an argument, was to bring up one of two subjects, either politics or religion. About the mid 1970's we added a third subject to this category, energy. My testimony today is directed at one form of energy, hydrogen, its use, and its potential for a much larger role in future energy systems of this nation, and the world.

Hydrogen is valuable as a fuel and as a chemical feedstock. The generation of hydrogen is equivalent to the storage of energy in chemical form. Hydrogen fuel can be used ultimately to produce thermal energy from combustion, and electrical energy from gas turbine generators and fuel cells. The use of hydrogen as a feedstock for ammonia fertilizer production is growing rapidly. An increased production of ammonia can serve two purposes. To grow food not only for consumption in the United States but for the rapidly growing world population, and it can also serve as an energy carrier by transporting this ammonia through existing ammonia pipelines to geographically dispersed locations, decomposing the ammonia to use its hydrogen content in fuel cells and produce both central and dispersed electric power supplies.

The production of hydrogen by electric utilities can add to their operating flexibility. Hydrogen generated by water electrolysis during times of relatively low consumer demand for electricity can be reconverted to electricity in a fuel cell or gas turbine during peak load periods. It also can be transported by pipeline for reconversion to electricity near the end user. Hydrogen can also be used as an alternative fuel as a substitute for or supplement to natural gas, and, most important, is an environmentally clean fuel. In its combustion there is no release of carbon dioxide, and no contaminants such as sulfur and nitrogen species, which are released in the combustion of fossil fuels and result in the so called acid rain experienced in many of our major industrial centers, are present in the combustion of hydrogen.

There is no fundamental problem banning the use of hydrogen as a heating fuel. In the days of manufactured gas from coal, the so called "town gas", which was essentially a mixture of hydrogen and carbon monoxide, was extensively used for heating and lighting.

Perhaps much longer term hydrogen could be a significant source of fuel in the transportation sector. As an example of its potential use in automotive engines, a major automobile manufacturer in Germany, Daimler-Benz, has been working since 1973 to adapt their standard automotive engines to burn pure hydrogen or a mixture of hydrogen and gasoline. In the near future they plan to demonstrate the practicality of the use of hydrogen as a substitute or supplemental automotive fuel by operating, initially, a fleet of 28 vehicles in the City of Berlin using town gas directly from the city's industrial and residential distribution network.

The basic technology for hydrogen distribution is well understood. Hydrogen can be transported in pipelines in substantially the same manner as natural gas. It can also be transported in various sizes of pressure vessels. An example of the latter are tube trailers used in over-the-road transport and the familiar gas cylinder used in laboratories and small industries. In larger quantities, hydrogen is transported as a cryogenic liquid in railroad tank cars and in tractor-trailer units.

During the heyday of the space programs in the 1960's and early 1970's very large (million gallon) liquid hydrogen storage facilities were constructed. The technical feasibility of storing hydrogen in metal hydrides such as titanium iron and magnesium nickel is also established.

In the U.S., production and use of hydrogen has increased by a factor of 40 since 1945 and has tripled in the last decade. The energy resources used to produce this hydrogen are natural gas about 73%, petroleum 23%, and about 1% miscellaneous sources. It's ironic that the most environmentally clean method to produce hydrogen water electrolysis, produces only a miniscule portion ($<$ 1%) of the total production in the U.S. Petroleum refining and chemical industries consume about 1/2 of the hydrogen produced, ammonia synthesis for fertilizer and general industrial use consumes another 1/3, and the production of methanol and miscellaneous usage consume the rest. Hydrogen is used to process the margarine we eat, to manufacture nylon for the clothing we wear, for pharmaceuticals, to cool utility generators, and for many other uses that form a part of our daily life, both industrial and personal.

This nations annual requirement for hydrogen is anticipated to grow substantially from the present approximately 1.4 quads of energy use (1.4 quads is equal to the energy in about 240 million barrels of oil) to a minimum of 5.5 quads (950 M B/O) by the year 2000, and to as high as 22 quads (3800M B/O) if hydrogen becomes a major factor in transportation fuel and the electric utility industry. A cause for concern for hydrogen planners is that, in face of such a range of increased demand, the availability of natural gas and oil to produce this hydrogen may be decreasing. The obvious consequence, if unconventional supplies of hydrogen are not developed in the interim period, is a serious shortfall of hydrogen to meet the increasing demand.

What would be the impact on the economy of this nation if we suffered an energy shortfall in the future? If, for example, we suffered say a 15% total energy shortfall over the period 1978-1985, the average annual growth rate of our gross national product would fall a full point. The cumulative effect would be about 435 billion in current year dollars. This same 15% total energy shortfall would also mean a decline in the average annual growth rate of business investment to the tune of approximately 160 billion also in current year dollars. This would also mean approximately 3 million fewer jobs available at a time when it is estimated that over the next ten years this nation has to create at least 10 million new jobs for the unemployed and for new people entering the work force. This would be a particularly painful result of an energy shortfall. An example of this type of pain was experienced during the natural gas shortfall during the winter of 1976-7. Approximately one million people were out of work for varying periods of time as a result of this, fortunately temporary, energy shortage.

In recognition of the need to develop methods of reduce the consumption of natural gas and oil, a major goal of the Department of Energy was established to develop technologies which permit substitution of renewable energy resources for natural gas and oil. The production of hydrogen from water using renewable energy resources such as solar, wind, hydroelectric, and ocean energy conversion systems is one technology being pursued. Water electrolysis systems would provide an excellent option for converting geographically dispersed renewable resources to a storable and transportable energy form.

In 1975 the General Electric Company was selected by the then ERDA as the contractor to develop an advanced electrolyzer technology, a spin-off from direct energy conversion technologies initially developed for the National Aeronautics and Space Administration for space applications in the 1960's. Since the original ERDA contract, in recognition of the potential for an expanded use of hydrogen in the future total energy picture, sponsorship of this development has grown significantly. In addition to the DOE and GE sponsorship, we now have a team in place that includes:

> Niagara Mohawk Power Corporation
>
> New York State Energy Research and Development Authority
>
> Empire State Electric Energy Research Corporation (who
>> represent a group of New York State Utilities)
>> Their interest is the use of off-peak hydroelectric power to store electrolytic hydrogen for electric power load management and, particularly in the case of Niagara Mohawk, a dual electric and gas utility, to supplement natural gas supplies.
>
> Gas Research Institute (who represent a group of gas utilities)
>> Longer term interest in the utilization of renewable power resources to generate electrolytic hydrogen for natural gas supplementation and to produce synthetic natural gas.

> Electric Power Research Institute (the technology development arm
> of the electric utility industry)
> Initial interest is to develop an advanced technology to produce
> hydrogen on-site for utility generator cooling.

Interest in the development of renewable energy resources is growing. One example is a development sponsored by the DOE Office of Solar Technology for extracting useful energy from the solar heat stored in vast surface waters of tropical and semi-tropical oceans. This Ocean Thermal Energy Conversion System (OTEC) will utilize the temperature difference in warm surface and cold sub-surface ocean water to power turbines and produce electricity. For OTEC platforms located reasonably close to a land mass, electrical energy could be cabled directly to shore. For those platforms located in ocean waters where it is impractical to directly transmit the electrical energy, an alternate energy carrier is required. One of the most cost effective energy carriers which can be used in this type of application is ammonia, produced from hydrogen generated by the electrolysis of water, and combined with nitrogen from the air. This ammonia energy can then be readily transported to any geographic location. I might add that many countries throughout the world such as France, Japan, West Germany and Sweden have expressed interest in, or are actively working on, OTEC concepts.

As an example of supplementing conventional energy, studies are being conducted by a major gas supplier to establish the feasibility of a large solar photovoltaic system to produce electrolytic hydrogen. The hydrogen so produced would be used to supplement their natural gas supplies.

Interest in renewable energy resources has also been expressed in Canada, Iceland, Greenland, Brazil, Africa, and Nepal, all of whom have excess hydroelectric power, and who are facing the need for increased ammonia production for fertilizer and, also, in many cases a need for synthetic fuels.

If I may summarize, hydrogen has a great deal of flexibility as a future fuel and as an energy carrier and energy storage medium. It can be produced from water using power from renewable resources. It is an environmentally clean fuel, thereby contributing to a reduction in the growing air pollution many of our major cities are faced with today. Hydrogen as a fuel will not only serve the growing energy needs of this nation, but is also capable of becoming an important factor in improving the U.S. balance of payments as an alternative to high cost imported oil and natural gas. The development of advanced technologies to produce and utilize hydrogen fuel, such as electrolyzers and fuel cells, is a critical element of this nations drive towards future energy independence.

F. T. O'Brien
Direct Energy Conversion Programs
General Electric Company

Biographical Sketch

Frank T. O'Brien

Mr. O'Brien, currently General Manager of the Direct Energy Conversion Programs Component of the General Electric Company, is a graduate of the U. S. Merchant Marine Academy, and has been employed by General Electric since 1955.

Prior to his service with GE, Mr. O'Brien held positions as Chief Marine Engineer, and Consultant, Marine Engineering. He also served as an Engineering Officer in the U. S. Navy.

During his service with GE, Mr. O'Brien held a variety of managerial assignments in Engineering, Marketing, Program Management, Technical Support Operations, and was appointed to his present position in 1969.

Mr. OTTINGER. Thank you very much, Dr. O'Brien. You are next Dr. Lindsey, accompanied by Dr. Nozik, and you may proceed as you see fit.

STATEMENT OF DR. HILDE LINDSEY

Dr. LINDSEY. Mr. Chairman, I appreciate the opportunity to testify this afternoon before the distinguished members of the Subcommittee on Energy Development and Applications and the Subcommittee on Energy Reserach and Production.

At the risk of repeating some of the points that have already been made, perhaps I should point out something that has not been stated explicitly so far this afternoon and, that is that much of the demand numbers for hydrogen that have been mentioned so far are for hydrogen as a chemical feedstock and not as a fuel.

Probably we should address this problem first, because this is the point where we can start to make an impact at our present technological development level. What I would like to say is that the demand growth for hydrogen is coming from two areas in the economy. It is coming from normal growth in for instance, ammonia and methanol production, and in the chemical's industry's use of hydrogen. It is also coming from the new demands that are being placed on such processes as petroleum refining, the new technologies that are having to be used because of the fact that the crudes are heavier and sourer these days.

Coal liquefaction, for example, will require four to six pounds of hydrogen for every hundred pounds of coal processed. That will be an enormous demand if we do opt for coal liquefaction.

The manufacturer of syngas to be used, for example, in methanol production, is going to involve loss of carbon if we use current technologies. If, however, we had an alternate source for hydrogen, we could preserve the precious carbon in the gas that is liberated into the atmosphere as carbon dioxide.

Several people have mentioned the possibility that electrical utilities are going to go to load leveling with fuel cells. Should this happen on an extensive basis, we would need one additional quad of hydrogen by 1990 because of that.

There are also new biomass technologies coming on line which are probably going to demand hydrogen in addition for their processing to fuels. In the foreseeable future there will always be a need for hydrogen as a chemical feedstock and should it prove possible to produce hydrogen economically on a large scale its versatility as a fuel and/or energy carrier could be exploited.

Hydrogen forming technologies in use today include steam reforming of methane, naptha, and other petroluem fractions partial oxidation of petroleum and other types of carbon sources; coal gasification; and water electrolysis.

Hydrogen produced via these methods markets between $25 and $200 per million Btu. (Now that is the merchant hydrogen. That's not the captive.) Conventional gaseous fuels currently cost $2 to $3 per million Btu and liquid fuel is $8 to $10 per million Btu. These market prices for hydrogen will continue to rise in response to the escalation in the cost of the feedstocks. It is hoped that by interfacing hydrogen production with solar technologies we would be able to solve the problem of producing hydrogen in sufficient volume and at prices which will permit us to take advantage both of its usefulness as a chemical feedstock and its flexibility and versatility as an energy carrier.

Among the solar-related technologies which have been suggested as means of producing hydrogen are wind, hydrothermal, falling water, and photovoltaics. In all of the above mentioned approaches, hydrogen would actually be generated via electrolysis and the solar technology has to be interfaced with the conventional or advanced electrolysis technology. Direct solar hydrogen production from renewable resources such as biomass and water is possible using photobiological, photoelectrolytic, and photochemical means. And these are the technological areas that I would like to address this afternoon.

For photobiological production of hydrogen I'm going to just sort of summarize off the cuff because this is the bulk of my report and to shorten things I will try to summarize. Many people are familiar with so-called biophotolysis which has been the use of blue-green algae to try to produce hydrogen. The production levels have been quite low for this particular algae. They are on the order of about 2 Btu's per gallon of cells per hour. This would amount to—if you had an acre of these things, not very deep, quite shallow—this would amount to about 7 million Btu's per gallon per day per acre of hydrogen.

Now there are some problems with blue-green algae. These algae grow in linear colonies called filaments and there are certain cells in these which are called heterocysts. They are very specialized, and they are the hydrogen producers. Normally the algae uses those cells to fix nitrogen as ammonium to feed to the other nonspecialized cells. If you force the algae to produce hydrogen without allowing it to grow it very soon kills the aglae. So you can't do this for extended periods of time on the same culture in the absence of growth. You have to change cultures.

It is possible that what you might want to do in this particular area is to focus more on production of ammonia fertilizer via this methodology or the isolation of a gene that you could transfer to other plants that would permit them to be able to make their own ammonia supply.

Now, green algae will also produce hydrogen at about the same level as blue-green algae. They have some of the same viability problems. They do not live under hydrogen producing conditions for long periods of time. However, if you cycle them through normal growth cycles and then into hydrogen production and then back out again, you could probably produce hydrogen this way. Again, the level of production is not very high, 2 Btu's per gallon per hour.

There is a system for producing hydrogen biologically which looks very promising, photosynthetic bacteria, which use the organics in waste streams to produce hydrogen at a level of about 20 Btu's per gallon per hour. Now, if you have an acre of those fellows, you can get 60 million Btu's per gallon per day out of an acre of them.

If you look at the waste stream resource right now there's about 0.6 quad of hydrogen out there in waste streams. By the year 2000 there will probably be a little over two quads with all the new waste streams that we envision coming into being. So if you wanted to in the short term, you should be able to use photosynthetic bacteria to produce enough hydrogen to make some impact on the present market for hydrogen. It is going to be very decentralized, but I won't try to address that question at this point.

Now, there are also so-called in vitro systems which are another approach to producing hydrogen biologically. And these in vitro systems, what one does is take photosynthetic components out of the cell, put them into artificial systems, and try to get them to produce hydrogen. It is possible to produce hydrogen in this manner. The work is very new—it has only been going on for a couple of years and the hydrogen production levels demonstrated are at about half the level of the photosynthetic bacteria, which is quite a high level of production for a solar technology right now. But this reaction doesn't represent true water splitting. Right now they are using organic redox carriers to produce hydrogen because they cannot couple it to the oxygen end of the reaction. As you probably know, in photosynthesis oxygen is produced at one end of the photosynthetic chair and hydrogen at the other. The oxygen portion of the reaction is not under control at all at this time. This is a promising area of research, but it probably should be funded on a basic level until some of the problems have been worked out.

I shall now consider the photoelectrolytic production of hydrogen. The conversion of solar energy to chemical energy via photoelectrolysis is an important long range option for meeting future energy needs. Protoelectrolysis is closely related to photovoltaic hydrogen production except that in photoelectrolysis the photoactive semiconductor material becomes not only the solar collector but the electrode as well; that is, it is in direct contact with the solution to be electrolyzed. Rather than having an interface between the production of electricity and the actual use of it to produce hydrogen, both processes take place at the same spot. This direct solar electrolysis of water is appealing because of its simplicity and because it avoids any loss in efficiency in establishing the interface between electricity generation and actual electrolysis. The maximum solar conversion efficiency for this system is estimated to be 25 percent.

There are some problems associated with this system at this time. Many semiconductor materials corrode under photoelectrolysis conditions. In addition, there is a difficulty in finding semiconductor materials which possess a wavelength threshold for absorption which overlaps well with the solar spectrum and compatible energetics with the two half-cell reactions in question.

This last point means that the photopotential produced in the semiconductor must be sufficient, for instance, to split water into hydrogen and oxygen. There is considerable interest in producing organic molecules instead of oxygen at the photoanode. Solutions to the above-mentioned deficiencies are being actively pursued via modification of existing semiconductor materials and development of totally new materials. The most promising seems to be in putting two semiconductors together so you can get good overlap for that particular reaction. The level of support in this area, however, is not sufficient if rapid progress is desired.

After only 4 years of research in this area, solar conversion efficiencies for photoelectrolysis of water stand at 1 to 2 percent. This corresponds to an instantaneous rate of 3.4 liters of H_2 per square meter per hour at high noon or an average yearly production rate of 51,000 liters of $H_2/m^2/yr$. If a yearly average production where one averages out winter, summer, et cetera, is taken the estimate is that you can produce about 520,000 Btu's per square meter per year at current efficiencies. That is well over what the photosynthetic bacteria will do—it is about twice the hydrogen production rate of photosynthetic bacteria now. However, if you use the theoretical maximum of 25 percent, the maximum amount of hydrogen which can be produced is 910 Btu's per meter squared per hour instantaneous.

Thirteen million would be the average yearly Btu's per meter squared. Most researchers in the field feel that if the support level were at least tripled, it should be possible to reach a 7-percent solar conversion efficiency which coupled with a materials cost of $70 to $80/m^2 would allow photoelectrolysis to be economically competitive with conventional electrolysis for hydrogen production by 1986. Commercialization then becomes a matter of bringing the new technology to production.

I shall now discuss photochemical production of hydrogen. The key to efficient photochemical conversion of solar energy to produce hydrogen involves effective collection of light causing the creation of positive and negative charges in the system. These charges must then be prevented from recombining before they take part in catalytic decomposition of water into hydrogen and oxygen. Chemical systems for converting sunlight to hydrogen based on electronic excitation can be divided broadly into two categories: homogeneous systems and those depending on interfacial systems.

The homogeneous systems for water catalysis, or water decomposition, have consisted in the past of looking at metal ions or their interaction with water and metal-halogen complexes where one part of the complex absorbs light and the other does not.

Systems involving transition-metal-ion-light accelerated reactions with water and metal-halogen photo-redox cycles have been studied, but such systems have very low solar conversion efficiencies. The most promising research in homogeneous photochemical water splitting involves work on transition metal complexes. The expense, liability, and low quantum efficiencies of the more promising of these complexes precludes commercialization efforts in the near future. However, these efforts should continue to be supported at a basic research level because of the inherent promise of such systems. They might possibly be able to reach 45 percent conversion efficiency at some point in the future.

Photochemical systems which show much promise are those which involve heterogeneous systems where the photochemical fuel producing reactions take place at the surface of a semiconductor or a micelle or membrane. The area where the most research is needed is in molecular architecture, that is to say, determining and engineering the needed geometrical relationship between the various components of the photochemical systems. In other words, how do you put them together in the right order so that they do what you want them to do?

It is here that the information gleaned from studying the manner in which the biological systems are constructed and energy is funneled through the structure may give invaluable information for solving molecular engineering problems.

The Swiss have recently announced a heterogeneous system which affects water dissociation. Pending patent decisions, the solar conversion efficiencies are not available for this process. An American firm is working with this Swiss group investigating commercialization potential. A number of other American firms have patents in this area which they are not actively pursuing at this time. The theoretical maximum for solar energy conversion in any photoconversion processes is about 45 percent.

However, real systems may not be able to achieve more than 25- to 35-percent solar conversion efficiencies. There is a long way to go to progress from present efficiencies to 25 percent solar conversion efficiencies, but persons in this field are confident that solar conversion efficiencies of 5 percent would be attainable by 1990 if the level of effort were properly supported.

In summary, the demand for hydrogen as a chemical feedstock is constantly growing in response to normal market growth and production of hydrogen intensive chemicals. Additionally, potentially enormous demands for hydrogen as an energy feedstock are developing principally from our commitment to synfuel production. The availability of hydrogen from renewable resources could substantially increase the yields of liquid fuels from such feedstocks as coal and/or biomass.

There would be a concomitant environmental benefit of more complete conversion of coal or biomass to liquid fuels—a reduction of levels of carbon dioxide released to the atmoshpere. Moreover, it is worth noting that the biological stripping of organic materials from wastestreams, that is by the photosynthetic bacteria, to produce hydrogen would also produce near tertiary quality water as an effluent.

A healthy solar hydrogen program would thus be a strategically important effort for a number of economic and environmental reasons, of which only a small number have been considered. It is a direct consequence of the low-funding levels for this and other hydrogen research that Europe and Japan have a substantial lead in developing advanced technologies for hydrogen production and use. Considering the potential significance and unquestionable value of a successful effort, it is surprising that the biomass and other DOE programs are planning to deemphasize an already meager effort.

Thank you for your attention, and I would welcome any questions.

[The prepared statement of Dr. Lindsey follows:]

Testimony of

Dr. Hilde Lindsey

The Solar Energy Research Institute

Before the

Subcommittee on Energy Development and
Applications
and the
Subcommittee on Energy Research
and Production
Committee on Science and Technology
U. S. House of Representatives
June 25, 1980

SOLAR HYDROGEN PRODUCTION SYSTEMS

The demand for hydrogen as a chemical feedstock in the U.S. is growing steadily. this growth is, in part, an expression of the normal increases in production of ammonia and methanol and augmented merchant use of hydrogen in commercial sectors such as the chemical, pharmaceutical, food, electronics, and metals industries. (See Figure 1.) The remaining portion of the growth in hydrogen demand arises from new technologies which are springing up in response to the current energy situation. A list of examples follows.

(1) In petroleum refining, two hydrogen intensive technologies, hydrotreating and desulfurization are becoming more common.

(2) Coal liquefaction is expected to require 4-6 lbs (725-1090 scf) of hydrogen for every 100 lbs of coal processed.

(3) Manufacture of syn gas for use in methanol production would involve less loss of carbon if needed additional hydrogen could be supplied from other sources.

(4) Should electrical utilities turn heavily to fuel cells for production of electricity and/or load leveling, the estimated hydrogen demand for this sector alone is projected to be 1 Quad by 1990.

(5) New biomass conversion technologies now being researched by SERI and others are also expected to contribute to the increased demand for hydrogen in the chemical processing which must be performed to transform these materials into fuels.

In the foreseeable future there will always be a need for hydrogen as a chemical feedstock, and should it prove possible to produce hydrogen economically on a large scale, its versatility as a fuel and/or energy carrier could also be exploited.

Hydrogen forming technologies in use today include steam reforming of methane, naptha, and other petroleum fractions; partial oxidation of petroleum, etc.; coal gasification; and water electrolysis. Hydrogen produced via these methods markets between $25 and $200 per million Btu (see Figure 2), while conventional gaseous fuels currently cost $2 to $3 per million Btu and liquid fuel $8 to $10 per million Btu. These market prices for hydrogen will continue to rise in response to escalation in the cost of the feedstocks from

FIGURE 1

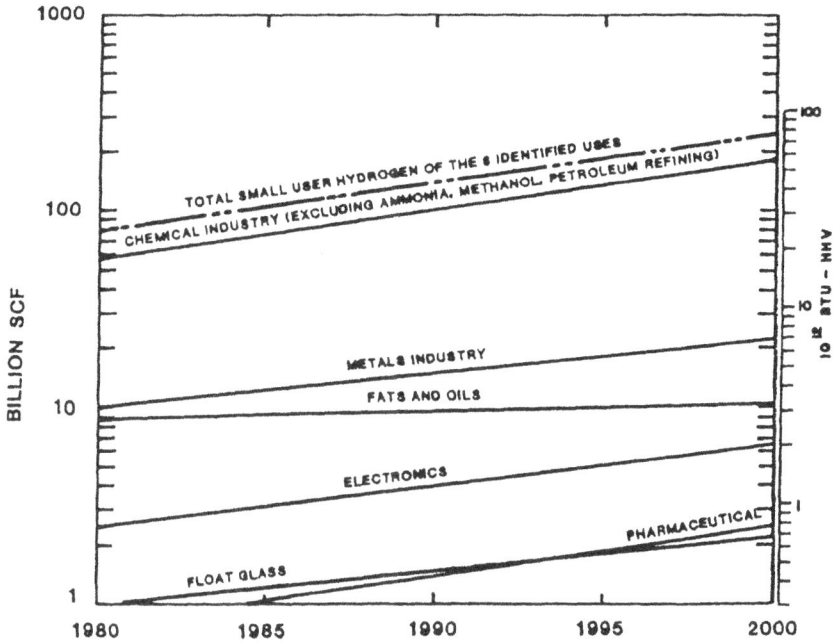

PROJECTED U.S. MARKET VOLUME FOR THE SIX
IDENTIFIED MAJOR SMALL USER HYDROGEN MARKETS:
1980-2000

Corneil, Hampton G., Heinzelmann, Fred J. and Nicholson, Edward
W.S., Economics of Small User Hydrogen, Proceedings of the
Symposium on Hydrogen for Energy Distribution, Institute of Gas
Technology, Chicago, Illinois, July 1978.

FIGURE 2

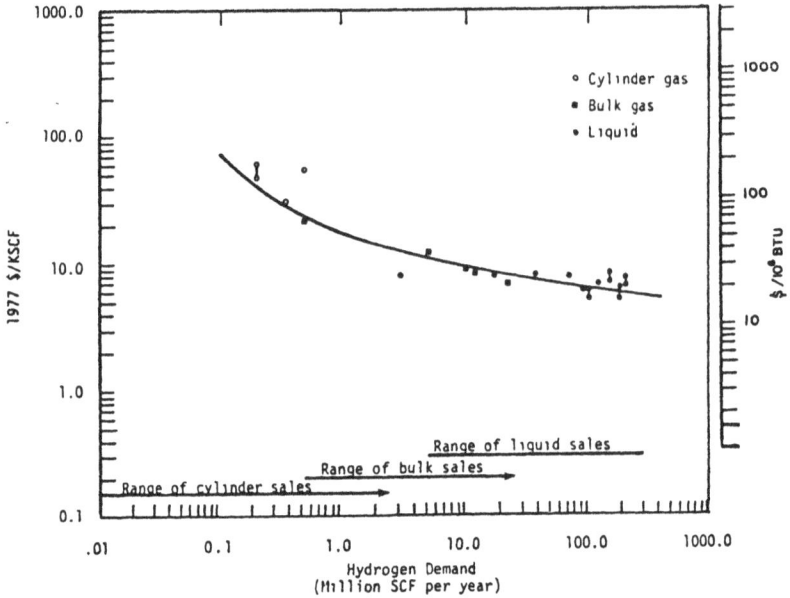

1977 MERCHANT HYDROGEN PRICES

The Market Potential for Electrolytic Hydrogen, Report Prepared
by the Futures Group, Glastonbury, Connecticut, for the Electric
Power Research Institute, EPRI Project No. 1086-4, Report No. EM-
1154, Palo Alto, California, August 1979.

which it is produced. It is hoped that interfacing hydrogen production with solar technologies will solve the problem of producing hydrogen in sufficient volumes and at prices which permit advantage to be taken of both its usefulness as a chemical feedstock and its flexibility and versatility as an energy carrier.

Among the solar-related technologies which have been suggested as means of producing hydrogen are wind, hydrothermal, falling water, and photovoltaics. In all of the above mentioned approaches, hydrogen would actually be generated via electrolysis, and the solar technology would need to be interfaced with conventional or advanced electrolysis technology. Direct solar hydrogen production from renewable resources such as biomass and water is possible using (1) photobiological, (2) photoelectrolytic, and (3) photochemical means. These are the technological areas which will be covered in this reveiw.

PHOTOBIOLOGICAL PRODUCTION OF HYDROGEN

There are several approaches which have been taken to photobiological hydrogen production which have involved photosynthetic bacteria (PSB), algae, and cell-free or in vitro systems. Photobiological hydrogen production is dependent on the presence of one or the other of two enzymes in the organisms which evolve hydrogen. These two enzymes are nitrogenase and hydrogenase. Hydrogen evolution in PSB and blue-green algae is due to nitrogenase. In green, red, and brown algae hydrogenase is the enzyme responsible for hydrogen evolution.

The evolution of hydrogen from blue-green algae has historically received the most attention and consequently is best known. There are two types of cells found in the filaments of the blue-green algae which produce hydrogen—vegetative (or normal growing and reproducing) cells and heterocysts. Heterocysts are specialized cells containing nitrogenase which have lost the normal photosynthetic capacities and exist only to provide the vegetative cells with ammonia needed for growth. (The normal function of the nitrogenase enzyme is to convert atmospheric nitrogen to ammonia.) On the other hand, the vegetative cells supply the heterocysts with the carbon sources necessary for its survival. If the blue-green algae is removed from contact with air, and hence, nitrogen, heterocysts produce hydrogen at a level of 20-40 microliters ($\mu\ell$) of hydrogen per milligram (mg) of dry cell weight per hour ($\mu\ell$ of H_2/mg dry wt/hr). Maintenance of the cells in the hydrogen producing mode eventually (in a period of about a month) costs the cells their viability. It is the opinion of the speaker that research in this system would probably best be directed toward enhancement of ammonia production for use as "algal fertilizer" and/or isolation of a transferable nitrogenase gene.

Photosynthetic bacteris (PSB) also evolve hydrogen using nitrogenase. As with the blue-green algae, a carbon source must be provided to the cells. However, it appears that these organisms can make use of the organic materials found in chemical, food processing, textile, paper, and municipal wastestreams to produce hydrogen. The rate of hydrogen production demonstrated for these organisms is   175   of H_2/mg dry wt/hr or, stated differently, for every pound of biological oxygen demand (BOD) consumed, approximately 30 standard cubic feet (scf) of hydrogen is produced. Appendix A-1 shows the amount of hydrogen which could conservatively be produced from wastestreams in 1980 and 2000. If the technology were currently available, it is conceivable that approximately 0.6 quads or roughly 40% of the present demand for hydrogen in the United States could be met. Hydrogen producing photosynthetic bacteria have been isolated and are well studied. The research into use of wastestreams to produce hydrogen is currently in the bench scale phase and is expected to be in the field by 1983 at a small-scale experimental level. If all goes well, a pilot plant is planned between 1987 and 1990. It should be possible to commercialize by 1995. By 2000 if sufficient commercialization has taken place, 1-3 Quads of hydrogen could be available from this source.

Green, red, and brown algae evolve hydrogen via the enzyme hydrogenase. These organisms are more evolutionarily advanced than those organisms which evolve hydrogen using nitrogenase. The biochemistry of hydrogenase hydrogen evolution is not well understood. Stated in everyday terms, this means that it is not yet clear whether the hydrogen produced is originating from water-splitting or reduced organics in the cell. This hydrogen evolution is also very oxygen sensitive, a problematic situation in photosynthetic organisms. Despite these drawbacks hydrogenase hydrogen evolution is extensively studied. Many of these studies will probably provide information which is most useful to molecular engineering for in vitro (cell-free) and/or photochemical systems for hydrogen production. Among those hydrogenase containing organisms studied here are green algae which will evolve oxygen and hydrogen silumtaneously under anaerobic conditions. The evolution rates are on the order of 450 to 700µℓ of H_2/mg chl/hr (less than 10% of the rate observed with PSB). This evolution rate slowly drops off after aproximately 8 hours, and if the algae are maintained in the hydrogen producing mode for longer than 24 hours, they begin to die. However, this biological water-splitting could presumably be carried out over long periods if the algae were allowed to grow normally between periods of hydrogen production.

Hydrogenase removed from the cell can also be used to produce hydrogen in artificial systems called in vitro systems. Photoproduction of hydrogen in in vitro systems requires the isolation of stable, photochemically active portions of the photosynthetic complex which interact with charge or electron carriers in such a way as to split water. An advantage of the in vitro systems is that they are independent of the energy-consuming metabolic processes of intact cells. Another is that the components of the in-vitro hydrogen producing system need not be isolated fromthe same organism. However, little is known about the individual components of this water splitting system and even less about how to organize the components. In addition, stabilization of the isolated, cell-free components is problematic. On the positive side, such in vitro systems have the potential for achieving the maximum theoretical quantum yield obtainable with intact cells, i.e., 10%. the evolution rates of hydrogen already achieved are approximately $10^4 µℓ$ of H_2/mg Bchl/hr. Unfortunately this hydrogen evolution was a demonstration of concept, not a demonstration of water-splitting. In any case, to date these rates have only been sustained for periods of less than 1 hour. Technologies based on in vitro systems are not expected to be commercializable before 2000.

PHOTOELECTROLYTIC PRODUCTION OF HYDROGEN

Conversion of solar energy to chemical energy via photoelectrolysis is an important long-range option for meeting future energy needs. Photoelectrolysis is closely related to photovoltaic hydrogen production except that in photoelectrolysis the photoactive semiconductor material becomes not only the solar collector but the electrode as well, i.e., it is in direct contact with the solution to be electrolyzed. This direct solar electrolysis of water is appealing because of its simplicity and because it avoids any loss in efficiency in establishing the interface between electricity generation and actual electrolysis. The maximum solar conversion efficiency for this system is estimated to be 25%. There are some problems associated with this system at this time. Many semiconductor materials corrode under photoelectrolysis conditions. In addition, there is a difficulty in finding semiconductor materials which posses a wavelength threshold for absorption which overlaps well with the solar spectrum and compatible energetics with the two half-cell reactions in question. This last point means that the photopotential produced in the semiconductor must be sufficient, for instance, to split water into hydrogen and oxygen. (There is considerable interest in producing organic molecules instead of oxygen at the photoanode.) Solutions to the above-mentioned deficiencies are being actively pursued via modification of existing semiconductor materials and development of totally new materials. The level of support is not, however, sufficient if rapid progress is to be made. For example, after 4 years of research in this area, solar conversion efficiencies for photoelectreolysis of water stand at 1-2%. (This corresponds to an instantaneous rate of 3.4 liters of H_2 per square meter per hour at high noon or an average yearly production rate of ~51,000 liters of $H_2/m^2/yr$). Most researchers in the field feel that if the support level were at least tripled, it should be possible to reach a 7% solar conversion efficiency which coupled with a materials cost of $70-$80/m^2 would allow photoelectrolysis to be economically competitive with conventional electrolysis for hydrogen production by 1986. Commercialization then becomes a matter of bringing the new technology to production.

PHOTOCHEMICAL PRODUCTION OF HYDROGEN

The key to efficient photochemical conversion of solar energy to produce hydrogen involves effective collection of light causing the creation of positive and negative charges in the system. These charges must then be prevented from recombining before they take part in catalytic decomposition of water into hydrogen and oxygen. Chemical systems for converting sunlight to hydrogen based on electronic excitation can be divided broadly into two categories: homogeneous systems and those depending on interfacial systems.

In homogeneous systems water is photochemically decomposed via metal ions and/or organometallic complexes. Systems involving transition-metal-ion-light-accelerated reactions with water and metal-halogen photo-redox cycles have been studied, but such systems have very low solar conversion efficiencies. The most promising research in homogeneous photochemical water splitting involves work on transition metal complexes. The expense, lability, and low quantum efficiencies of the more promising of these complexes precludes commercialization efforts in the near future. However, these efforts should continue to be supported at a basic research level because of the inherent promise of such systems.

Photochemical systems which show much promise are those which involve heterogeneous systems where the photochemical fuel producing reactions take place at the surface of a semiconductor or a micelle or membrane. The area where the most research is needed is in molecular architecture, that is to say, determining and engineering the needed geometrical relationship between the various components of the photochemical system. It is here that the information gleaned from studying the manner in which the biological systems are constructed and energy is funneled through the structure may prove invaluable in solving molecular engineering problems. The Swiss have recently announced a heterogeneous system which affects water dissociation. Pending patent decisions, the solar conversion efficiencies are not available for this process pending patent decisions. An American firm is working with this Swiss group investigating commercialization potential. A number of other American firms have patents in this area which they are not actively pursuing at this time. The theoretical maximum for solar energy conversion in any photoconversion processes is about 45%. However, real systems may not be able to achieve more than 25-35% solar conversion efficiencies. There is a long way to go to progress from present efficiencies to 25% solar conversion efficiencies, but persons in this field are confident that solar conversion efficiencies of 5% would be attainable by 1990 if the level of effort were properly supported.

SUMMARY

The demand for hydrogen as a <u>chemical feedstock</u> is constantly growing in response to normal market growth and production of hydrogen intensive chemicals. Additional, potentially enormous, demands for hydrogen as an <u>energy feedstock</u> are developing principally from our commitment to syn fuel production. The availability of hydrogen from renewable resources could substantially increase the yields of liquid fuels from such feedstocks as coal and/or biomass. There would be a concomitant environmental benefit of more complete conversion of coal or biomass to liquid fuels—a reduction of levels of carbon dioxide released to the atmosphere. Moreover, it is worth noting that the biological stripping of organic materials from wastestreams to produce hydrogen would also produce near tertiary quality water as an effluent.

A healthy solar hydrogen program would thus be a strategically important effort for a number of economic and environmental reasons, of which only a small number have been considered. It is a direct consequence of the low funding levels for this and other hydrogen research that Europe and Japan have a substantial lead in developing advanced technologies for hydrogen production and use. Considering the potential significance and unquestionable value of a successful effort, it is surprising that the Biomass and other DOE programs are planning to de-emphasize an already meager effort.

APPENDICES

RESOURCE BASE	ESTIMATED ANNUAL QUANTITY AVAILABLE		ESTIMATED ANNUAL HYDROGEN PRODUCTION POTENTIAL	
	1980	2000	1980	2000
Municipal Sewage (based on BOD of digestor effluent) [a]	7.5 x 10^9 lbs BOD [b]	9.2 x 10^9 lbs BOD [c]	2.9 x 10^11 scf H_2 [d] (0.094 Quads)	3.5 x 10^11 scf H_2 [e] (0.11 Quads)
Food Processing Wastes	5.7 x 10^9 lbs BOD	6.9 x 10^9 lbs BOD [e]	2.2 x 10^11 scf H_2 (0.065 Quads)	2.7 x 10^11 scf H_2 (0.081 Quads)
Stillage	6.2 x 10^8 lbs BOD		2.4 x 10^10 scf H_2 (0.007 Quads)	
Textile Process Wastes [f]	1.9 x 10^9 lbs BOD	5.0 x 10^9 lbs BOD [g]	7.2 x 10^10 scf H_2 (0.022 Quads)	1.9 x 10^11 scf H_2 (0.057 Quads)
Paper Process Wastes [h]	1.2 x 10^10 lbs BOD	3.3 x 10^10 lbs BOD [g]	4.5 x 10^11 scf H_2 (0.136 Quads)	1.2 x 10^12 scf H_2 (0.361 Quads)
Chemical Process Wastes [i]	2.0 x 10^10 lbs BOD	5.3 x 10^10 lbs BOD [j]	7.6 x 10^11 scf H_2 (0.229 Quads)	2.0 x 10^12 scf H_2 (0.607 Quads)
TOTALS	4.8 x 10^10 lbs BOD	1.1 x 10^11 lbs BOD	1.8 x 10^12 scf H_2 (0.545 Quads)	4.0 x 10^12 scf H_2 (1.20 Quads)

a) Denver figures
b) represents 25% of total biomass available
c) assuming avg biomass composition and $C(H_2O)$ + $H_2O \xrightarrow{PSB} 2H_2 + CO_2$
d) assuming an average of 300 Btu/scf H_2
e) assuming an annual growth rate of 1%
f) good deal of cellulosic waste, may wish engineer PSB to digest cellulose or do preliminary treatment, digestion or fermentation

g) assuming an annual growth rate of 5%
h) also large amounts of cellulose and heavy metals, toxicity of this stream unknown
i) plastics manufacturing main contributor to this stream, toxicity unknown

APPENDIX A-1

56

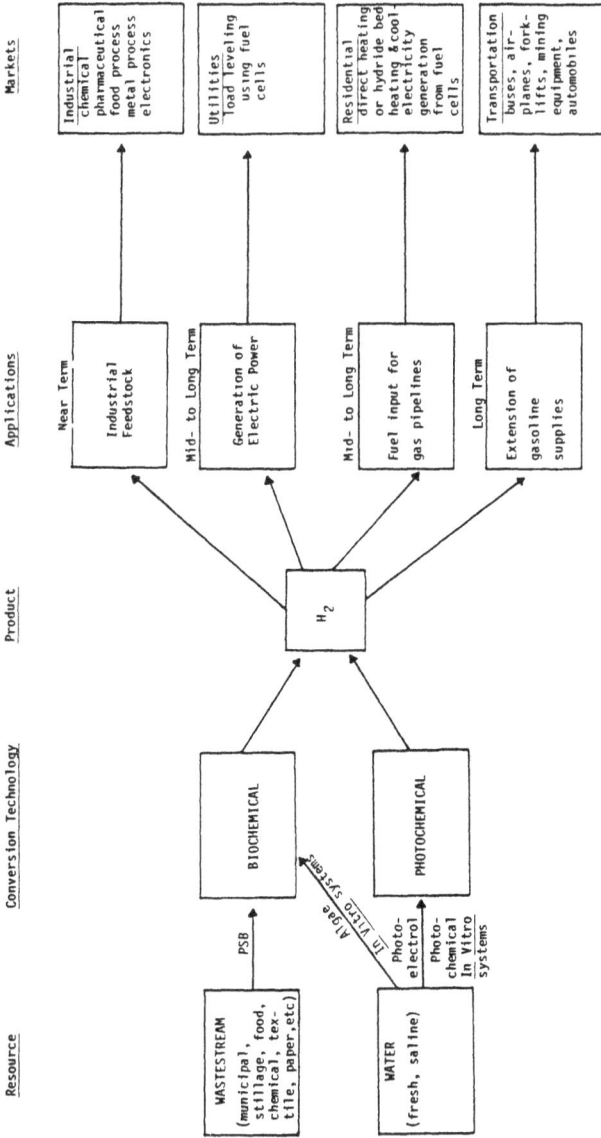

APPENDIX A-2

ELECTRICITY TRANSMISSION COSTS

Data	Value Assumed
Average cost of five 500-kV lines built since 1969 – includes right-of-way, excludes cost of one urban line	$130,000/mile
Cost of d c. line at 0 65 times the cost of comparable a.c. line	$84,500/mile
Typical power capability of 500-KV line	900,000 kW
Typical a c. terminal cost	$8/kW
Typical d c. terminal cost	$30/kW
Average 500-kV overhead line cost	$0.144/kW-mile
Average 500-kV overhead line cost	$42.32/$10^6$ Btu-hr-mile
Average d.c. overhead line cost	$0.093/kW-mile
Average d.c. overhead line cost	$27 50/$10^6$ Btu-hr-mile
Cost of two terminals for a.c.	$16/kW
Cost of two terminals for a.c.	$4,687/$10^6$ Btu-hr
Cost of two terminals for d.c.	$60/kW
Cost of two terminals for d c.	$17,580/$10^6$ Btu-hr
Cost ratio of underground to overhead power transmission	10:1 to 40·1
Cost of underground line	$1.44/kW-mile
Cost of underground line	$423 2/$10^6$ Btu-hr-mile
Total overhead line plus terminal costs for 200 miles	$0.112/kW-mile
Total underground line plus terminal costs for 200 miles	$1.68/kW-mile
Projected cost for 138,000-V superconducting line for 10 miles	$0.88/kW-mile $0.60/kW-mile
Projected cost of 345,000-V superconducting line for 10 miles	$0 20/kW-mile

D.P Gregory, assisted by P.J Anderson, R J Dufour, R H Elkins, W J D. Escher, R B. Foster, G M Long, J Wurm & G G Yie, 'A Hydrogen-Energy System', prepared for the American Gas Association by the Institute of Gas Technology, Chicago, August 1972, p. X-22.

APPENDIX A-3

58

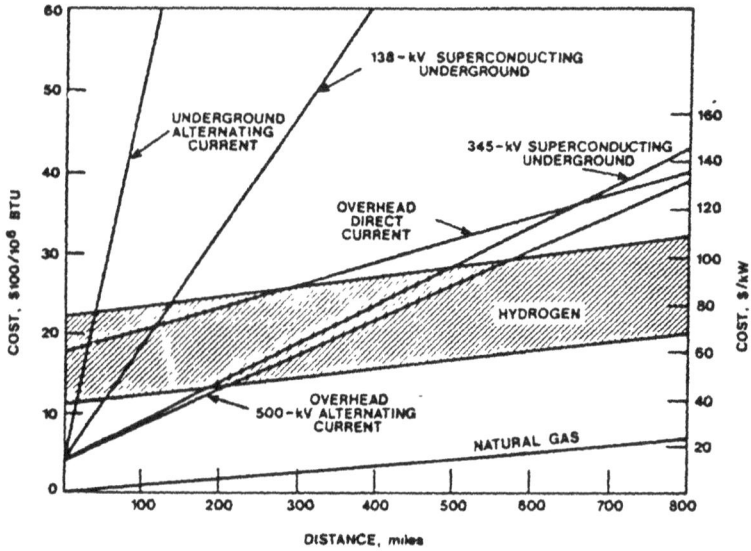

Cost of energy transmission facilities.

Reference same as for Appendix A-3, p. X-23.

APPENDIX A-4

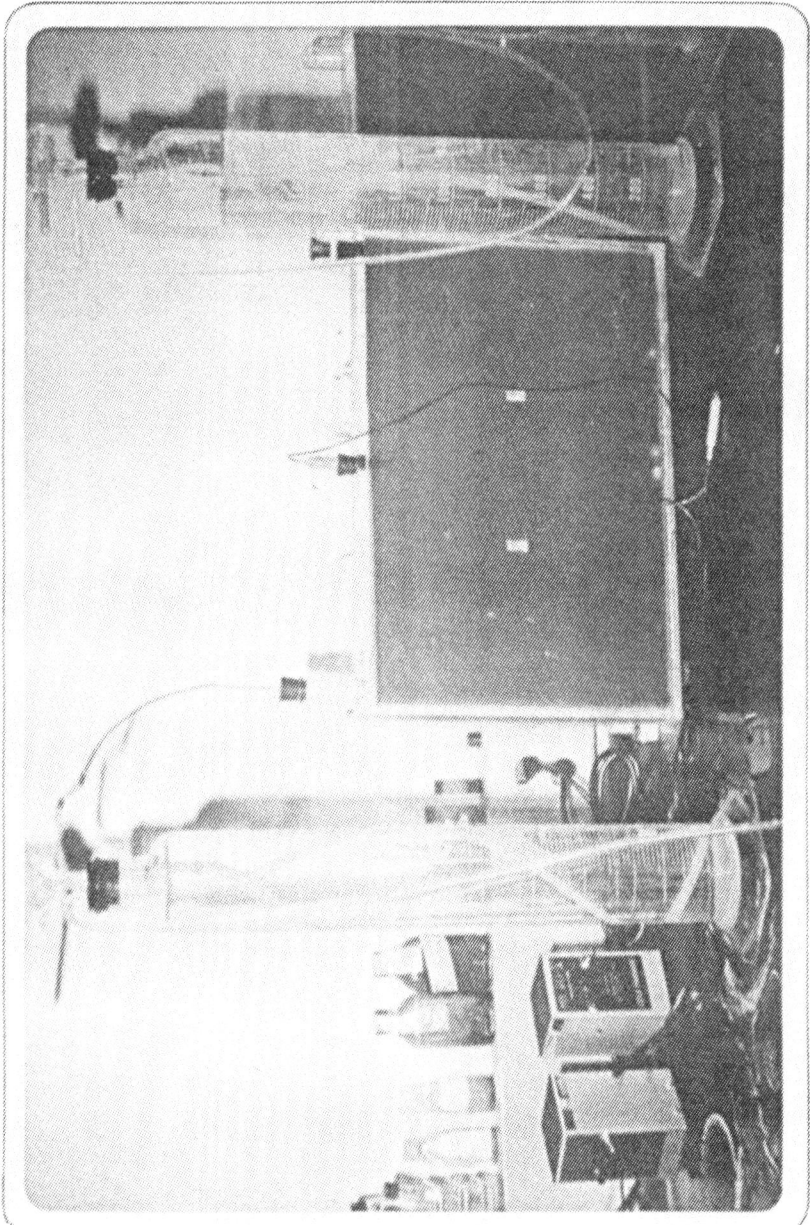

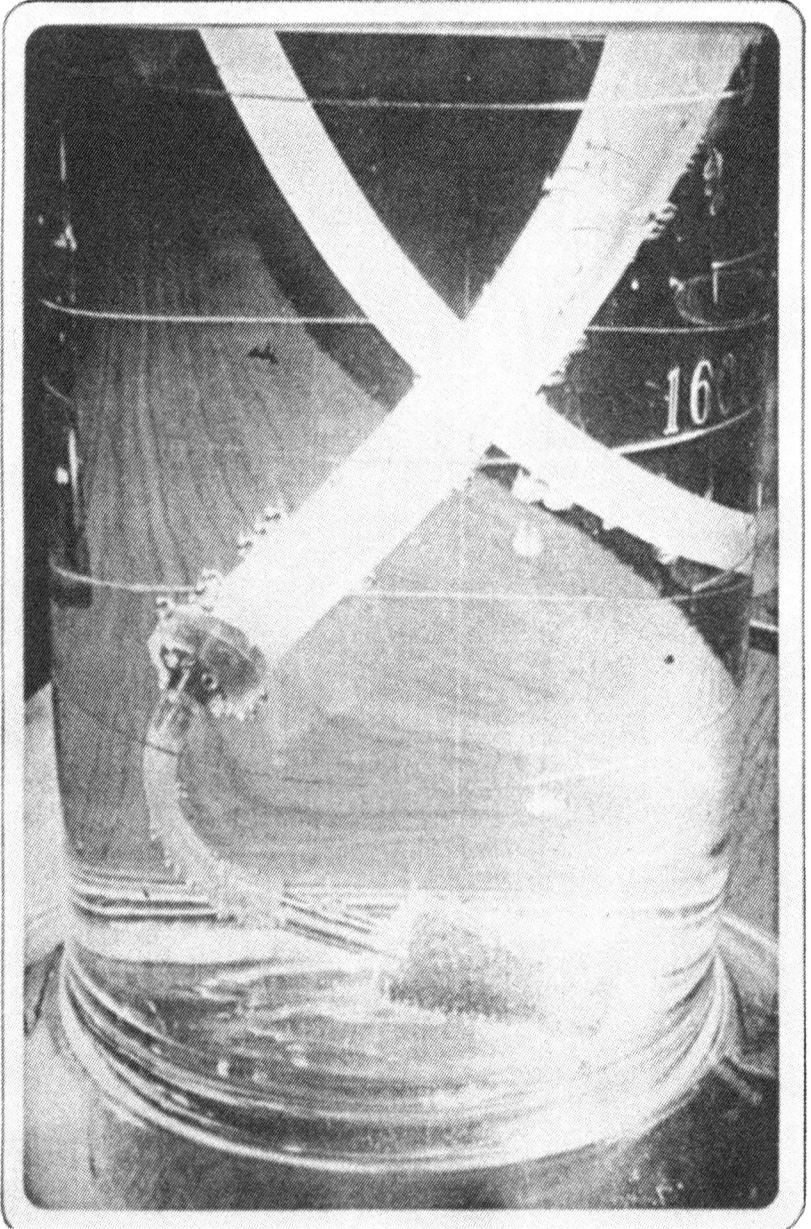

Energy Storage via Vesicles

Bilayer vesicle: "hydrocarbon shell"

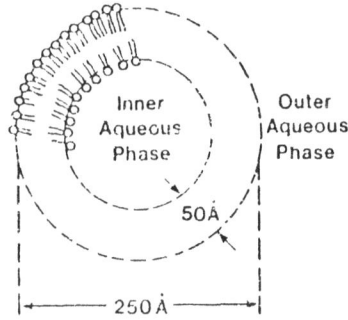

If H_2 produced in inner aqueous phase and O_2 formed in outer aqueous phase

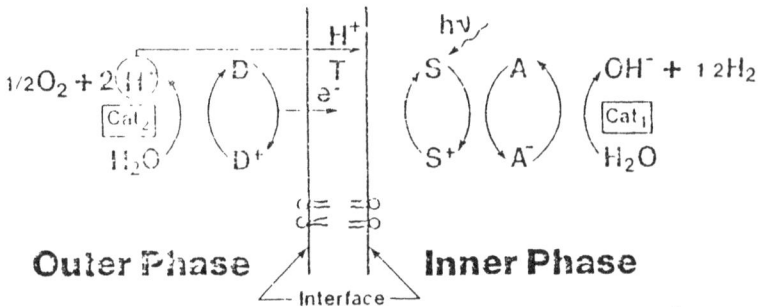

Outer Phase   Inner Phase

D = Organometallic Complex
Cat_2 = Metal Oxides
T = Quinones

$A = CH_3 - \overset{+}{N}(O)-(O)\overset{+}{N} - CH_3$
$S = Ru(bipy)_3^{2+}$
$Cat_1 = PtO_2, \dots$

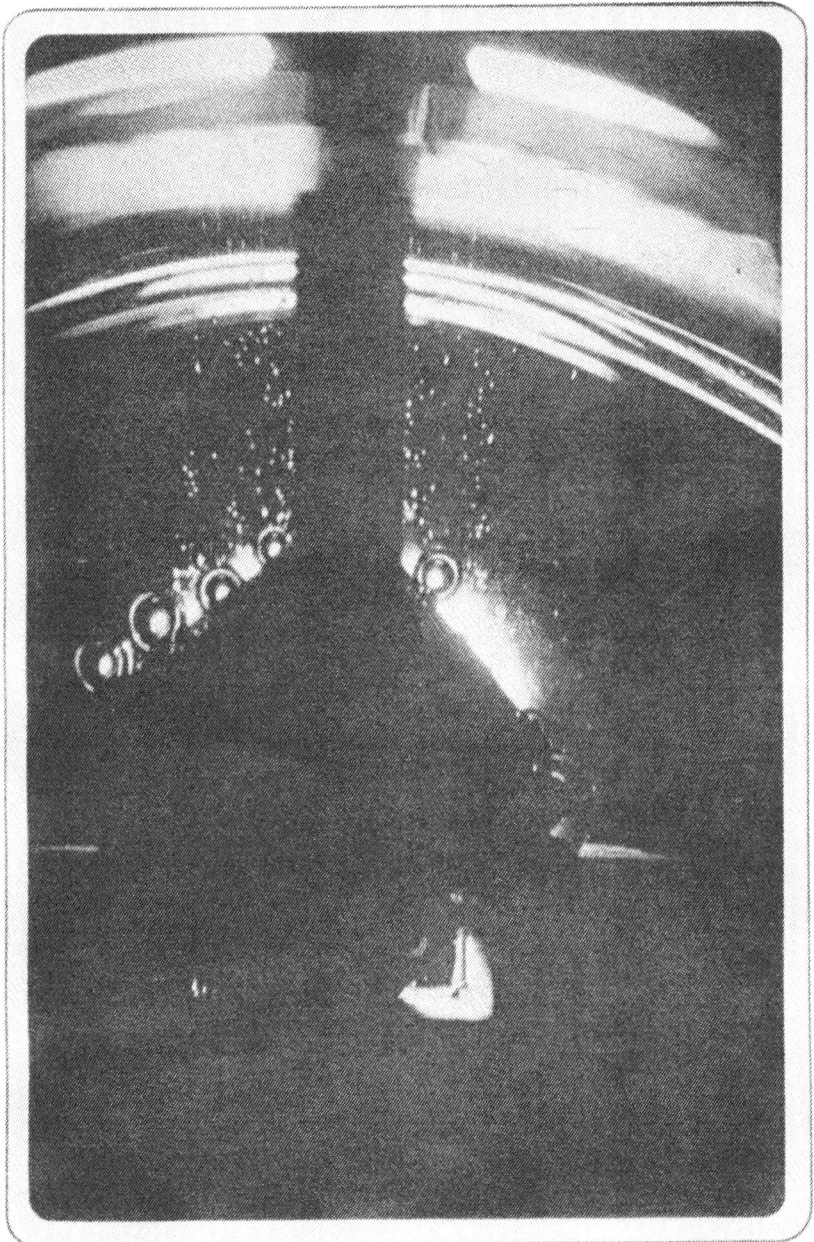

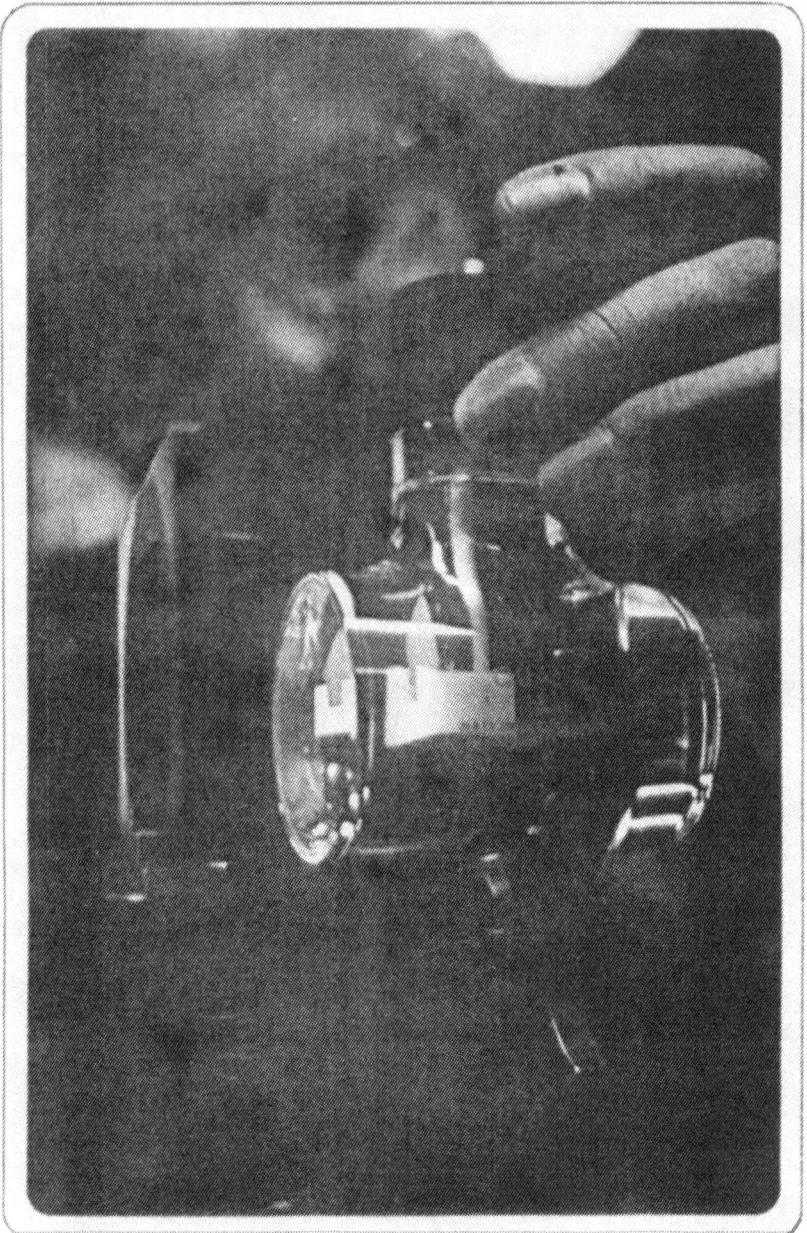

Mr. OTTINGER. Thank you very much.

Let me get on the record—and I don't know whether you can do it or whether we should wait for Dr. Kane. What is the DOE's present level of effort in hydrogen research, do you know?

Dr. LINDSEY. In what area, sir? There are several hydrogen areas covered in various branches of DOE.

Mr. OTTINGER. If you can give it all to us, fine, or if you want to supply it for the record, that will be fine.

Dr. LINDSEY. I think I should probably supply it for the record.

[The material follows:]

In response to Congressman Ottinger's question regarding DOE's present level of effort in hydrogen research, I refer the Congressman to the table entitled "Expenditures on Hydrogren Research" submitted by Dr. Kane in his testimony.

Mr. OTTINGER. What is SERI's involvement at the present time?

Dr. LINDSEY. SERI is involved in solar hydrogen production. We are involved in this sort of advanced or avant-garde type of research which I have just described to you.

Mr. OTTINGER. What are the dollars and numbers of people that you have?

Dr. NOZIK. I might be able to shed some light on that. SERI has an in-house research program which is carried out in the branch called Photoconversion in which there are approximately 15 full-time scientists and 5 visiting scientists, a total of about 20 researchers investigating all of these 3 areas that Dr. Lindsey mentioned. The budget for fiscal year 1980 was approximately $1.3 million. Then in addition to the internal research there is a small effort in supporting similar work outside of SERI which Dr. Lindsey manages and which I believe is a little less than $1 million.

Dr. LINDSEY. A lot less than $1 million, about $600,000. So the total in-house and out-house research funding would be about $2 million, or a little under.

Mr. OTTINGER. Is there private research going on in this area to any considerable extent?

Dr. NOZIK. Yes. There is quite a bit of interest in the private commercial sector. In the country. I think many of the chemical, electronic, and oil companies do have programs in hydrogen production by these methods. It is a very active research area generally.

Mr. OTTINGER. Is GE doing anything in this, Dr. O'Brien?

Dr. O'BRIEN. Yes; they are. Our people in Philadelphia in the advanced energy areas are doing work in solar, photovoltaic, wind biomass, and they are involved in all potential methods of renewable energy resources.

Mr. OTTINGER. Do you know what level of effort GE is maintaining?

Dr. O'BRIEN. I honestly don't.

Mr. OTTINGER. Could you let us know?

Dr. O'BRIEN. Yes; we can get that for you.

Mr. OTTINGER. Dr. Lindsey, you conclude your statement by saying there is not nearly enough being done in this area and what has been done is being reduced. Do you have any recommendations for us as to what kind of level of effort would be needed to pursue this to its full potential?

66

Dr. LINDSEY. From the persons I have spoken to in the field that are active in the research, I think that the level of funding—I will correct this if it is incorrect—currently throughout the United States in, for instance, photoelectrolysis is about $1 million as far as DOE programs are concerned.

As far as the photobiological funding, it is at about the same level. Apparently, photochemistry is about at the same level, so the total would be about $3 million. Most people in the field feel that with a little more money—for instance—triple the current budget it would be possible to make much more rapid progress toward the goals.

Mr. OTTINGER. Has anybody in DOE actually tried to devise a program aggressively pursuing the research?

Dr. NOZIK. I think the main focus of that research resides in the Office of Energy Research and perhaps Dr. Kane could address that.

Mr. OTTINGER. Let me recognize now my colleagues in order of their appearance for questions, except that we will take Mr. McCormack first since he is cochairing the hearings.

Mr. McCORMACK. Thank you, Mr. Chairman.

I want to congratulate the witnesses for their testimony. I have several questions and I want to sort of jump from one to the other of the witnesses.

Dr. Funk, you mentioned in your testimony, in your point 4 of your five major points—

[Reading from Dr. Funk's statement:]

The high temperature heat source which provides the heat for thermochemical processes * * *

As I understand it, the higher the temperature, the higher the efficiency of these systems, up to 500° to 700°C; is that correct?

Dr. FUNK. Yes, sir.

Mr. McCORMACK. So what we really need are two levels of research here. One is how to best use the heat that we have, that is, in our nuclear powerplants and in our coal-fired plants to produce hydrogen with thermochemical systems, on the one hand, and then research on the other systems such as the organic systems that have been mentioned by Dr. Lindsey. Do you see this as a correct perspective? We really have almost two complete regimes here, one where we have a great deal of energy available to us to use now, the dump heat from our existing electrical generation plants on the one hand. We have to figure out a way to use this heat with high-temperature systems, as compared to the more long-range research on the organic systems.

Would this be a fair appraisal would you think?

Dr. FUNK. Yes; I think it is a fair appraisal. In one case, the energy is generally quite diffuse in the systems that Dr. Lindsey is discussing. In thermochemical systems, the energy is quite highly concentrated. It is sort of the same kind of difference as you find in trying to use solar energy in one case and energy derived from combustion or nuclear fission in another case.

Mr. McCORMACK. So then one main line of research should be in the dissociation of water in a thermochemical system, where heat is essential. That would be one main line of research.

Dr. FUNK. Yes.

Mr. McCORMACK. I would like to switch over to Dr. O'Brien for a moment. You mentioned the transport of hydrogen for use in fuel cells or gas turbines during peak loading. It is my recollection that natural gas is the cheapest source of energy to move about. It is substantially cheaper to move energy as natural gas than it is as electricity.

Dr. O'BRIEN. When you say the cheapest form——

Mr. McCORMACK. Per unit of energy.

Dr. O'BRIEN. I really don't know. Of course, there are existing natural gas lines all over the United States. So to transport hydrogen in those same lines is a question that has not been answered because, as you know, the molecules of hydrogen are much smaller than natural gas and the potential for leakage, therefore, would be greater.

Mr. McCORMACK. This is what I wanted to get at. You said on page 2 that hydrogen can be transported in pipelines in substantially the same manner as natural gas. Now previously in testimony before this committee several years ago, we heard testimony to the effect that in all likelihood hydrogen could be transported in standard existing pipelines if the valves and pumps were replaced with specially adapted equipment to handle the hydrogen. Do you know anything about that and would you care to comment?

Dr. O'BRIEN. Well, GE did some testing where one of the sponsors of a DOE prime sponsored program, the development of an advanced electrolyzer technology is also cosponsored by the Niagara-Mohawk Power Corp., Empire State Electrical Energy Research Corp., New York State Energy Research & Development Authority, Gas Research Institute, GE, and so forth, and one of the tests we performed in our laboratory for Niagara-Mohawk was that they took up a section of pipe from their gas transmission lines and I believe—I can confirm this—that the pipe was at least 50 years old—we tested it. We could find no leakage or migration through this old pipe of the hydrogen. What we were completely unable to do is to seal the old flanges they had on it.

I have not seen any recent data by Niagara-Mohawk, so I really cannot talk for them, but their plan was, and I believe still is, to supplement their natural gas supply about 10 percent with hydrogen in their existing pipelines. And I have not seen any recent evidence to the contrary that they have given up on that concept.

Mr. McCORMACK. There is no problem with hydrogen embrittlement at these temperatures, I take it.

Dr. O'BRIEN. That's always a question, but again in the pipe that we tested—and it was not an extensive test program, but we did not find any.

Mr. McCORMACK. Are there any tests going on now where hydrogen is being pumped through pipes and valves, which has been going on for a year or two, at ambient temperatures or higher?

Dr. O'BRIEN. We are doing nothing. I really can't state whether anybody else is.

Mr. McCORMACK. It strikes me this would be an important area of research.

Dr. O'BRIEN. Yes, it is; and I believe Sandia was doing some work in this area.

Mr. McCORMACK. If any other witness has anything on that, we can pick it up when the time comes.

Mr. OTTINGER. It is possible that Dr. Gregory from IGA, who will testify shortly, will have something on that.

Mr. McCormack. Dr. O'Brien, you also said that the production of hydrogen has increased by a factor of 40 since 1945.

Dr. O'Brien. Yes.

Mr. McCormack. How is most of the hydrogen being produced today?

Dr. O'Brien. Roughly 75 percent is natural gas.

Mr. McCormack. How is it dissociated?

Dr. O'Brien. Steam reforming.

Mr. McCormack. Are you getting carbon dioxide?

Dr. O'Brien. You are getting some carbon dioxide. You are getting about 80- to 85-percent purity of hydrogen.

Mr. McCormack. Are they throwing away the carbon dioxide then?

Dr. O'Brien. In most cases, yes. Depending on the location of the reformer and the needs of the industry in that area, they could conceivably find a use for the carbon dioxide.

Mr. McCormack. Finally, in your discussion of OTEC systems you mentioned using ammonia as a mechanism for transporting hydrogen. I am concerned whether or not you have explored the possibility of transporting ammonia simply adsorbed on an iron-titanium surface?

Dr. O'Brien. It can be done in that manner. I think for the OTEC concept, however, where the plan would be to electrolyze water to produce the hydrogen and then mixing with nitrogen from the air, you are going to be making bulk quantities of ammonia and the most cost effective method of transporting that would be by vessel rather than storing in hydrides. I think it would be much more expensive to transport it in hydrides.

Mr. McCormack. Has anybody explored the comparison of total systems here? In one instance you have to use the hydrogen after you combine it with nitrogen to make ammonia. You go through that step, then you have to have refrigerated ships to transport ammonia as compared to simply adsorbing the hydrogen on iron-titanium surfaces and then handling them as bulk solids at ambient temperature.

Dr. O'Brien. I can't answer that, Mr. McCormack. I'm sure in the various studies that have been made by OTEC from an economic standpoint, particularly those studies made by Johns Hopkins Applied Physics Laboratory, I am sure they would have considered that option.

Mr. McCormack. Thank you very much. We will have to check into that some more with them.

Finally, if I may, Dr. Lindsey, you said that direct photoelectrolysis from water is appealing because of its simplicity and because it avoids any loss in efficiency in establishing an interface between electricity generation and actual electrolysis. Why is this so?

Dr. Lindsey. I think I will let Dr. Nozik respond to this one. I have some opinions, but they're just opinions.

Dr. Nozik. Well, there are a couple of answers to that question: One is that the latter process, taking a photovoltaic device and coupling it to electrolysis, involves a two-step operation and there's an efficiency loss with each step, such that when you look at the total system, the total net theoretical efficiency of that two-step process is about 15 percent.

This number is derived by multiplying the efficiency of photovoltaics times the efficiency of electrolysis.

Photoelectrolysis is a one-step system, so that the effective voltage that is developed and the electrolysis that ensues occurs in one step. The estimated upper limit efficiency there is about 25 percent. You see there is a substantial increase in the attainable efficiency in the one-step photoelectrolysis process over the two-step process involving photovoltaics cells coupled to electrolysis cells.

Mr. McCormack. Is this theoretical?

Dr. Nozik. This is theoretical; the 25 percent is a theoretical number.

Mr. McCormack. The 25 percent is also a theoretical number, as you know, for photovoltaics.

Dr. Nozik. Then you have to take that 25 percent and multiply it by the efficiency of the electrolysis step itself, which I believe currently runs about 60 to 70 percent. Now in addition to that, you have much more flexibility with photoelectrolysis in the configurations of the devices. In particular, it is possible to configure photoelectrolysis cells which consist of very fine particles. They are miniature cells which could be suspended in a slurry as a colloid and that opens up a whole range of new and different types of solar reactor designs which have potential engineering advantages over the former system, which would involve the use of photovoltaic arrays coupled to electrolysis.

And then, finally, there is the possibility of doing novel chemistry. The semiconductors can act as very unique photocatalysts and drive reactions on the surface, photocatalytic reactions, which you could not achieve in the other systems. So I think by virtue of these three advantages it is worthwhile to pursue research in photoelectrolysis.

Mr. Ottinger. Will the gentleman yield for a second?

Mr. McCormack. Yes.

Mr. Ottinger. What kind of efficiencies is Texas Instruments projecting from its current research?

Dr. Nozik. I think they are projecting something on the order of 6 percent. I think they have about four or five percent right now. They think they could make this competitive at 6, 7, or 8 percent. Now the Texas Instruments approach is a two-step process. That kind of approach fits into this latter category of using particulates, but it is through an array system. They make solar cells in the form of very fine particles and these are imbedded in a matrix and it becomes a planer array. The array absorbs light and produces electricity in the cells themselves, but it is still a two-step process, because the semiconductor is coated with a metal and then you have the electrolysis step following the photovoltaic step.

Mr. Ottinger. Are they directly connected?

Dr. Nozik. You never withdraw current directly from the fine particles. The electricity is produced in these micron-sized spheres and the metal coating acts as an electrode. An electrolysis reaction proceeds on the surface of the particles and produces hydrogen and an oxidized halogen. Then you collect these gases and store them and feed them back to a fuel cell later to recover electricity.

Mr. Ottinger. Thank you.

Mr. McCormack. I have a couple more questions here. I will be very quick. Again, Dr. Lindsey, you commented that with availability of hydrogen from renewable resources for synfuels production there would be a concomitant environmental benefit—a reduction of levels of carbon dioxide released to the atmosphere. This leads to my question: Wouldn't it be better if you were working with systems that didn't involve the use of carbon at all so you could keep the carbon dioxide or carbon monoxide systems completely out and reduce that environmental hazard and work with water?

Dr. LINDSEY. That would be lovely if it were practical at this time. Unfortunately, it seems to me we are going to have to face the fact that we are going to have to use synfuels. It is possible I am not answering your question. I may not have understood.

Mr. McCORMACK. Are there any biological systems that use solar energy without producing carbon dioxide or carbon monoxide?

Dr. LINDSEY. Oh, I see what you mean. The biological system does produce carbon dioxide as well as hydrogen. It turns out that carbon dioxide is a desirable commodity these days. There is a firm in Colorado which is now selling carbon dioxide to Texas to use for a solvent in reclaiming oil from wells that can't be reclaimed by normal methods. It turns out that CO_2 under pressure is a very desirable solvent.

Mr. McCORMACK. I am delighted that somebody has found a use for it. You recognize, of course, that really our most fundamental environmental problem that we are facing is the release of carbon dioxide into the atmosphere, which is involved in the burning of any fossil fuel at all.

Dr. LINDSEY. That's very correct.

Mr. McCORMACK. If we are really going to solve our energy and environmental problems, we must get away from burning any fossil fuels.

Dr. LINDSEY. Eventually. I wish I could say it is coming quickly, but I don't believe it will. I believe we will have to probably live with it for a while.

Mr. McCORMACK. Unfortunately, that's true, and I hope we're not too late. You mentioned that Europe and Japan have a substantial lead in developing advanced technologies for hydrogen production and use, specifically what areas of technology?

Dr. LINDSEY. I should have brought those examples along. I'm afraid they are in the form of some abstracts that I have back in my office and if you will permit me, I will respond to that question in writing.

[The material referred to follows:]

In response to Congressman McCormack's question regarding Europe and Japan's leadership in hydrogen production and use, this leadership expresses itself must clearly in the level of funding and the close cooperation between government and industry. Japan is pushing solar hydrogen production. Honda and co-workers in 1972 were the first persons to demonstrate the practicability of the concept of photoelectrolysis. There continues to be a high level of interest in this and other solar hydrogen production technological develpment in Japan. Eurpe has a very strong program in photochemical processes and probably has a research lead in this field at this time. This is substantiated by the recent announcement of a Swiss group headed by a gentleman named Graetzel that they had succesfully split water photochemically. In Germany. Daimler-Benz has a very active program of research and development for hydrogen use as a fuel in buses and automobiles and a smaller program in use of hydrogen residentially for heating (hydride bed exchange) and cooking. The success of the Daimler-Benz effort is demonstrated by the fact that they have hydrogen buses and cars in the prototype stage and contract with West Berlin to supply a fleet of hydrogen buses.

Mr. McCORMACK. We would be delighted to have you provide them.
Mr. OTTINGER. Mr. Blanchard?

Mr. BLANCHARD. Mr. Chairman, I have been in and out while the testimony has been going on, and I wouldn't want to interrupt what chain of thought has been developed, but I would like to reserve the right to ask a question or two after the others who have been here.

Mr. OTTINGER. Mr. Gore?

Mr. GORE. Thank you, Mr. Chairman. I won't take very long. I want to thank the witnesses for being here. I have a strong interest in this field and sponsored an amendment in conference to S. 932, the Omnibus Energy Act, to include hydrogen from water in the definition of synfuels, thus, making it eligible for the substantial benefits contained in that legislation which will be voted on the floor of the House tomorrow and it is scheduled to be signed into law by the President on July 4.

In light of those provisions, Mr. Chairman, I think that the legislation which is pending and was described at the beginning of these hearings may involve some duplication of what the conference bill already accomplishes. I'm wondering if any of our panelists are familiar with the S. 932 provision and if they share my opinions on that?

Mr. McCORMACK. In the absence of any comment from the panel, will the gentleman yield?

Mr. GORE. Yes.

Mr. McCORMACK. We are not considering any specific legislation. Congressman Grassley did testify on this bill, but there is no specific legislation being considered.

Mr. GORE. I am aware of that, but the first witness described legislation in some detail and I'm wondering, Dr. O'Brien, are you familiar with the provisions in the conference committee bill?

Dr. O'BRIEN. What was that number again?

Mr. GORE. S. 932.

Dr. O'BRIEN. No; I am not.

Mr. GORE. OK. What is the state of hydrogen development in other countries? Which other countries are moving faster than the United States in this field?

Dr. O'BRIEN. In the production of hydrogen in a particular manner?

Mr. GORE. Yes.

Dr. O'BRIEN. Everybody is working—when I say everybody, I think all of the so-called free world nations are actively working on evaluating all of the renewable resources to obtain energy to produce hydrogen by various methods. Now one interest I have is in electrolytic hydrogen.

In the United States, as you perhaps know, the Department of Energy, plus the industry members I have mentioned previously, are all supporting an advanced electrolyzer concept that General Electric developed as a spinoff from space-age technology in the sixties. And the European Community, they are actively looking at the standard alkaline electrolysis, the liquid electrolyte, which has been around for a long time but primarily in areas of the world where there was very inexpensive hydroelectric power. They are looking to advance the standard technology while the United States is looking at a new technology to improve the efficiency of electrolyzers and thereby reduce the cost for producing a unit of production.

I would say, to try and answer your question, I think everybody is looking at advanced technologies and my personal feeling is—obviously, I'm biased—I think the advanced technology being sponsored by Department of Energy has a leg up, but we've still got a long way to go and the level of support required to take this technology to a point where it can be commercialized by industry, it is not moving fast enough.

And if we are looking at trying to provide an alternative energy source to either supplement natural gas, we have the ocean thermal consideration, all of these things are going to require a technology to take the energy produced and to convert it to a useful product. There is where we are lacking in direction and support from a time standpoint.

Otherwise this thing will be going on to the nineties and we need it today.

Mr. GORE. I am wondering, Dr. Lindsey, if you are familiar with the recent study performed for the Department of Energy by the Billings Energy Corp. on hydrogen from coal.

Dr. LINDSEY. No. I can't say that I am.

Mr. GORE. Are any of the witnesses familiar with that study.

Dr. FUNK. I was chairman of the review group that observed that study.

Mr. GORE. What are your comments on it, Dr. Funk? My reaction was that it should have provoked a major reevaluation of the economics of that particular process. Do you agree?

Dr. FUNK. I think the numbers quoted in that study could stand some close scrutiny. Those numbers are for very large plants and the economy of scale factored into the numbers. I think they may be low by as much as a factor of two in terms of a practically realizable hydrogen-from-coal plant today.

As I recall, those numbers were about $4 or $4.50 per million Btu. A number line seven or eight might be more reasonable for hydrogen from coal today.

Mr. GORE. In your view, is that the only explanation for the big discrepancy between the numbers that were produced in that study and the numbers that were produced in the previous landmark work on that subject from Exxon?

Dr. FUNK. Are you referring to the work that Exxon did which they subcontracted to Chem Systems?

Mr. GORE. It was my understanding that prior to this recent study that was really the only work that the Department had done or contracted on this approach.

Dr. FUNK. I would say that the numbers produced by Exxon were done in substantially more detail than the work done by DOE and Billings. The Exxon study, as I recall, involved Coppers-Totzek technology, which is state-of-the-art technology. All the costs involved were included. I think the discrepancy between the Exxon numbers and the Billings numbers lies in, as I have said earlier, the size of the plant. I believe the Billings plants were much larger than the Exxon plants and there were other favorable assumptions.

Mr. GORE. Are you familiar with the different projected profit per unit of production in the two studies?

Dr. FUNK. The Exxon report assumed 100-percent equity financing and a 20-percent return on capital. Some of the Billings studies, at any rate, involve utility financing with 75–25 debt/equity and a lower return on capital——

Mr. GORE. Do you remember what the return on capital was?

Dr. FUNK. I do not.

Mr. GORE. It is my understanding—and I would like to submit additional material for the record on this——

Mr. OTTINGER. Without objection, it is so ordered.

Mr. GORE. That item was responsible for most of the difference in the numbers. The profit figure built into the Exxon study was just enormous and when you isolated that factor and took another view of the size of the profit to be expected out of this technology, then the cost was changed rather dramatically.

Dr. FUNK. The development of a production cost figure is always complicated by the method of financing and the return required. That is why it makes more sense to look at the direct capital cost of the plant per unit of output and the thermal efficiency of the plant. Then you can go to the production cost in whatever way you like.

Mr. OTTINGER. Will the gentleman yield?

Mr. GORE. Yes.

Mr. OTTINGER. Why would one find it preferable to go from coal to hydrogen rather than going from coal to methanol.

Dr. FUNK. For end use requirements that hydrogen might serve that methanol would not.

Mr. GORE. And the end use efficiencies are significantly higher are they not?

Mr. OTTINGER. We have a huge potential market with ethanol, so I would think that one could make a similar argument for methanol.

Dr. FUNK. One of the end uses for the hydrogen produced from coal in the Billings work was to run buses in the Allegheny County Port Authority in Pittsburgh, Pa. Those folks were very interested in running their buses on hydrogen and not on methanol. They were interested in knowing what it would cost to build coal gasification plants to produce the hydrogen for their particular end use.

Mr. OTTINGER. Wouldn't it be much cheaper to go from the coal to methanol or methane than it would to hydrogen?

Dr. FUNK. I don't believe so.

Mr. OTTINGER. I don't believe so.

Mr. OTTINGER. Are there any cost comparisons available there?

Dr. FUNK. I'm sure there are. I cannot quote them for you directly. The Exxon report that has been referred to has those costs.

Mr. GORE. Does it make sense to assume 100-percent equity financing? Does that give you a realistic picture of the economics?

Dr. FUNK. I guess it depends on whose realism you are interested in. If the chemical industry is going to build a plant today, it may well be built with 100-percent equity financing and they may derive the return they wish.

Mr. GORE. It would seem to me that if you build in these kinds of assumptions, if you build in an assumption, No. 1, of 100-percent equity financing, No. 2, of just an absolutely ridiculous profit figure, then the result is going to be expectably pessimistic. Am I going wrong there?

Dr. FUNK. I don't believe the return numbers used by Exxon were ridiculously high. They looked for a 20-percent return. And I think that is not all that unusual in the chemical industry. I don't think there is any way to decide the question of how the financing should be done, which is why it makes more sense for comparison purposes to work with the direct capital cost of the plant per unit of output and the efficiency, rather than going to a production cost figure.

Mr. GORE. Nevertheless, the result in that study led to a prevailing pessimism about the hydrogen production throughout the Department of Energy for quite some time; is that not the case?

Dr. FUNK. I don't know the answer to that question.

Mr. GORE. In retrospect, do you believe that the figures Exxon produced were far too pessimistic?

Dr. FUNK. No. I believe the numbers in that Exxon report are quite good for the assumptions used to make the numbers.

Mr. GORE. Well, for the assumptions they used to make the numbers, you are choosing your words very carefully, and the question I'm asking, though, is if one were seeking a real world view of how promising this particular hydrogen technology is, one would be misled into being more pessimistic than one should be, if one relied on the Exxon study; correct?

Dr. FUNK. Possibly, if the entire job were to be done on an industrial basis. If there are other factors to be introduced into the financing, then the picture is different. If we expect industry to move into the hydrogen production business, they will have to have the kind of numbers you see in that Exxon report. If there are other financial arrangements, such as loan guarantees or purchase agreements or ability to do municipal-type financing, then the picture will be different.

Mr. GORE. Thank you, Mr. Chairman. And I thank all of the witnesses.

Mr. OTTINGER. I ask my question because I have seen a National Academy of Sciences study which indicates that the cost per million Btu of hydrogen from coal would be about $9.50 and methane from coal is $6. There's a substantial disparity. Are those figures off or are they on a different basis than the figures from the Exxon study?

Dr. FUNK. I'm sorry, I cannot recall those numbers.

Mr. OTTINGER. Could you take a look at that for us and help us out for the record?

Dr. FUNK. Sure.

Mr. OTTINGER. Mr. Forsythe?

Mr. FORSYTHE. I apologize for not having been able to be here to hear all the witnesses. I would like to ask a couple of questions. And this one is for the panel rather than for any individual. This does go back to the bill which we heard about but are not considering presently. The concept that was involved, as I understand it, is to arrive at the goal of this developing hydrogen technology through incentives, loan guarantees and tax benefits rather than public financing. Do you think this is a situation in which we need to have R. & D. or is it a matter of economic incentives so far as industry is concerned?

At least I know Dr. Funk would be on one side and Dr. Nozik and Dr. Lindsey on the other, so Dr. Funk, how about that problem? To get this technology on line, can it be done by industry with incentives and loan guarantees, et cetera, or do we have to have the research and development still continue at a major pace?

Dr. FUNK. I believe there is a lot of research and development needed to be done before this technology will come on line. I think there will have to be incentives before it will come into the market-place.

Mr. FORSYTHE. You have to have the egg before you can hatch a chicken.

Dr. Lindsey, I assume is going to agree now.

Dr. LINDSEY. I do agree with his statement, yes. There is a study which has just been published which JPL did for DOE studying market penetration for solar hydrogen. They considered the more conventional solar hydrogen, not the technologies I presented today, that is, OTEC and other hydrothermal, falling water, and wind, etc. Their conclusions after their studies were that in order to get any penetration of this technology there would have to be incentives, because of the risk involved and because of the current climate in the commercial sector.

Mr. FORSYTHE. Let me try to penetrate that a little bit. I've heard it said here that the investment in research has been not adequate and that I assume is referring to DOE or the Federal Government's investment in research. You are not telling me that incentives would replace that, are you?

Dr. LINDSEY. I may not be using the right word. What do you feel I mean by incentive, then maybe I can respond to the question.

I think I may have misunderstood your question. What do you feel that I mean by incentive?

Mr. FORSYTHE. Tax incentives for private industry, loan guarantees and this type of thing but without spending more at the Federal level for research and development?

Dr. LINDSEY. No; you are going to need research in order to bring the technologies to maturity.

Mr. FORSYTHE. In other words, we are technology limited?

Dr. LINDSEY. Yes.

Mr. FORSYTHE. Will incentives penetrate the market?

Dr. LINDSEY. That depends on what you are talking about. If you are talking about electrolysis, it's probably a different story. But if you are talking about solar, any kind, we are technologically limited. Electrolysis is somewhat separate. It provides a technology interface with many of the solar technologies for producing hydrogen, and it is in a state of readiness. There is no technological holdup. It could be improved, but it is definitely technologically ready and has been used for many years.

Mr. FORSYTHE. Thank you very much.

Mr. OTTINGER. Mr. Dornan?

We have a couple of minutes and then we have to go to vote.

Mr. DORNAN. Maybe if I could just submit my questions then for the record for a written response because we do have this vote.

If we use hydrogen as a fuel for propulsion of cars and aircraft, how much more is it going to cost compared to synthetic fuels? This is a big issue and close to home in my district, southern California.

How much change, really basic change, is going to be required in the motor systems?

Can we make conversions of existing fleets or are we really going to have to deal with fleet replacements for buses, automobiles, and aircraft?

When do you think in the foreseeable future we would try to fly a cryogenically cooled, liquid hydrogen aircraft?

From the National Research Council report, I see that the cost of hydrogen from electrolysis is two or three times as much as the cost of the other synthetic fuels for propulsion; say, gasoline produced from shale or from coal. I have three questions on this:

Why is that cost higher? Is it just fundamentally higher, or if it is a technological deficiency, is there some way it can be reduced?

Isn't electrolysis of water by nuclear- or coal-generated electricity a hope for liquid fuels for the future?

Thank you, Mr. Chairman.

Mr. OTTINGER. I would certainly like to hear some of the answers to those, but I think we will have to go vote. We will let Dr. Kane try his hand at those questions I think. The report which I referred to from which we are getting these figures, for your help, Dr. Funk, is a report called "Hydrogen as a Fuel" by the Hydrogen Panel of the Committee on Advanced Energy Storage Systems, Energy Engineering Board, Assembly of National Engineering Research Councils, published by the National Academy of Sciences.

We thank you all for your assistance to the committee. We will excuse this panel and we will resume with the next panel as soon as we finish the vote. Thank you very much for your help.

[Answers to questions from Mr. Dornan follow:]

I am unclear as to what Congressman Dornan wishes to imply by "really basic change" in motor systems so I will respond by reiterating the answers to Congressman Dornan's questions given me by a colleague, Joe Finegold, at SERI.

The changes which must be performed to convert an automobile or bus from gasoline to hydrogen combustion are:

(1) The induction system should ideally consist of either a timed fuel injection system for gaseous fuel or a dual intake valve system, although a simple gaseous carburetor (e.g. propane) can be used.

(2) In engine tuning, the air/fuel ratio and spark advance need to be appropriately adjusted.

There are some engine modifications which are desirable but not necessary. They are as follows:

(1) In burning hydrogen it is desirable to use a higher compression ratio to increase engine efficiency.

(2) The valve timing and ignition systems should be optimized for hydrogen in order to maximize engine performance.

(3) The cooling passages of the engine should be redesigned to minimize backfiring.

(4) It may be desirable to change the combustion chamber to improve efficiency and/or performance.

Conversion of existing fleets of automobiles and buses is possible. However, some retrofits have been more successful than others, for example, compare the highly successful Mercedes-Benz hydrogen vehicles with the problem-plagued Riverside, California bus. The most difficult retrofit problem is the fuel system. Hydrides are bulky expensive, and heavy. Liquid hydorgen is bulky and expensive. Most automobile can neither tolerate the extra weight of hydrides nor provide tank space for liquid hydrogen in these days of emphasis of fuel economy. For captive fleets of buses and short-range truck fleets and even taxis retrofitting for hydrogen is probebly technically feasible. On the other hand, current aircraft design does not include sufficient fuel space for liquid hydrogen and, hence, airline fleets would probably not land themselves to retrofit programs.

As early as the late 1950's Pratt and Whitney converted aircraft engines to burn liquid hydrogen and even went as far as to flight test one engine. Many liquid hydrogen fuel systems have been developed and flown by NASA for rocket applications. Development of liquid hydrogen propelled aircraft is probably not a particularly risky venture. An international ad hoc committee is currently working on a technical development program for hydrogen aircraft. The first flight test for the aircraft is planned for 1985. With additional funding this schedule could be significantly compressed.

The current cost of hydrogen produced via electrolysis probably reflects two influences. One has to do with the low market demand for electrolytic quality hydrogen (average purity—99.9 percent). What I'm trying to say is that currently electrolytic hydrogen is a specialty product. The other factor influencing the price of electrolytic hydrogen is the price of electricity from which it is generated. The inherent low efficiencies of the electrical generation process which is tide to a heat engine and the increasing market and environmental cost of the feedstock for its generation make for expensive electricity and hence expensive hydrogen. Electrolysis itself is a mature and efficient technology. This fact cannot, however, overcome the limitations in efficiency and feedstock costs which preceed the eltctrolysis step. If one wishes to produce hydrogen electrolytically using currently available technology, one should use hydroelectric power.

The efficiency bottleneck encountered with generating electricity via heat engines can be overcome to some extent by using electricity produced using solar technologies such as OTEC, wind and photovolaics to generate electrolytic hydrogen. However, materls costs and technological immaturity currently render hydrogen produced in this manner more expensive than that produced by conventional electrolysis. Ultimately, the means of choice for hydrogen production could be photoelectrolytic and photochemical because of higher efficiencies possible and because the water dissociation is accomplished directly with out electrolysis. However, this means of producing hydrogen is not commercially available at this time, and much research and development will be necessary in order to bring the technology to maturity.

Mr. OTTINGER. We will resume our hearings with the second panel consisting of Dr. Derek Gregory, vice president for engineering research, Institute of Gas Technology, Chicago, Ill.; Dr. Al Mezzina, program manager, hydrogen energy storage program, Brookhaven National Laboratory, Upton, Long Island, N.Y.; and Dr. James Kane, Associate Director for Basic Energy Sciences, Office of Energy Research, U.S. Department of Energy; accompanied by Dr. James Swisher, Director, Division of Mechanical and Chemical Storage, Office of Advanced Conservation Technologies, and Dr. F. Dee Stevenson, Chief, Process and Techniques Branch, Division of Chemical Sciences.

Why don't we start off with Dr. Gregory?

STATEMENT OF DR. DEREK GREGORY

Dr. GREGORY. Thank you. It is an honor and a privilege to be here to talk to you today. Hydrogen is a very broad subject. There are many applications of hydrogen use and to try to present a statement in a few moments, I want to tell the committee the primary reason why we at IGT are interested in hydrogen as a fuel, comment on the status of these developments as I see them today, and point out some changes in the energy situation that, in my opinion, have modified the time scale of the introduction of hydrogen.

I would like to comment upon the position now taken at IGT and the gas industry through the Gas Research Institute and make some comments on the position taken by the National Research Council committee of which I was privileged to be a member.

First, the interest in hydrogen, the real primary interest in hydrogen, is an ultimate replacement for natural gas. I want to confine my major talking and thinking to that particular application. One of these days we will have to rely less on fossil fuels and more on nonfossil fuels and the major choices, of course, are solar and nuclear. These cannot always be harnessed at the end user's premises so we need a means of storage. Electricity is the obvious choice but not the only choice. Compared to oil and gas today the transportation of electricity is more expensive, less efficient, and more ugly looking. If we can make synthetic oil or gas from nuclear and solar, this would be able to be transported in the existing transportation system. If we try to make a synthetic hydrocarbon, we need a carbon supply as well as a hydrogen supply. The technical and energy problems involved in nonfossil carbon are such that it is easier to make hydrogen than synthetic hydrocarbons, if you are limited to nonfossil sources.

If hydrogen can be transmitted in the natural gas delivery system that is already in use and burned in appliances that are already in use, it seems it would be a lot better than replacing everything with electric equipment.

Hydrogen is not a source of energy although it is often confused as being a source. It is a carrier just like electricity. It needs energy to produce it from water and it gives most of that energy back when you burn the hydrogen. On burning the hydrogen the only combustion product is steam. There is no carbon, smoke, or carcinogens. It is the cleanest fuel known to man.

We hear a lot of the good news about hydrogen, but there is some bad news attached to it as well. Where have we got to after 10 years of fairly intensive research in the United States and in other countries? The electrolysis of water is commercially available today and has been for some time. Great strides have been made in improving its cost and its efficiency. Many thermochemical cycles have been invented and tested and two laboratories have operated cycles running continuously using electric heat to simulate nuclear and solar energy. Efficiencies of 40 or 50 percent are being predicted and checked out in the lab with some confidence.

Biological and solar radiation processes to produce hydrogen from water have been demonstrated to work but they are still at a basic developmental stage and it is too early to project costs. Hydrogen has been shown to be compatible with natural gas distribution equipment. That is, in the low pressure equipment that is under the streets of our cities and the gas meters in our homes. Promising results have been obtained in testing hydrogen in high pressure transmission lines. There were no surprises found, but there is still some doubt about the safety of welds at high pressures.

Tests have not been carried out for a long enough time to be convincing in my opinion. For example, the tests we ran at IGT on distribution equipment were concluded after 6 months' exposure and we would like to see longer tests run.

Mr. OTTINGER. Why were they concluded?

Dr. GREGORY. The contract ended.

Mr. OTTINGER. Is that DOE?

Dr. GREGORY. Yes.

The seasonal storage of hydrogen in underground formations appears to be possible and storage as a metal hydrite is feasible for certain short-term applications. Hydrogen can be mixed with natural gas and burned in conventional appliances up to about 15 percent by volume before the appliances start giving trouble. More than 15 percent hydrogen requires some adjustment or modification of burners.

Over the past 5 years there have been some changes that have occurred that have affected the time scale of hydrogen. The slowdown of nuclear development we have seen means that providing an alternative carrier for nuclear energy is not so urgent. However, solar development is now being emphasized and hydrogen can perform the same storage and transmission function for solar energy. This is even more important for solar than it is for nuclear. So we have seen a lowering of emphasis of the urgency for nuclear transmission, but a buildup in the interest of using hydrogen as a means of moving solar energy. The development of unconventional natural gas and of substitute natural gas made from coal, shale, and biomass promises to make large amounts of methane gas available at prices below those predicted for nonfossil hydrogen.

We don't think we can make hydrogen from nuclear or solar energy for much less than something in the $6 to $12 per million Btu range. We can produce lots of hydrocarbon fuels in that price range. However, energy changes occur rapidly and unpredictably and since hydrogen is the only chemical fuel available from materials that are in unlimited abundance and which can be produced for almost any energy source, it should remain on our active project list.

IGT's position at the present time is that we have found no major technical obstacles to the replacement of natural gas with hydrogen at some time in the future. We continue to regard hydrogen as a long-term insurance policy rather than a near-term requirement. Retaining much of the natural gas transmission distribution and utilization equipment is good for the Nation, because it will result in more economic service to the consumer in the long run than transition to an all-electric delivery system.

The major technical problems are in the production of hydrogen and particularly in the cost and the efficiency of production. More long-range research is needed in this area and we must also be sure about the compatibility of transmission pipelines.

Hydrogen as an automobile fuel looks attractive. The weight and performance of a hydrogen car would appear to be better than that of an electric car. However, we must have a readily available refueling system for hydrogen. You can plug in an electric car almost anywhere, but you can't buy hydrogen at the corner gas station. And it is the refueling and delivery system that would seem to be the most difficult part of the hydrogen automobile in the future. Making hydrogen from coal is technically available today, but we believe that it will be always more expensive and less efficient to make hydrogen than SNG or methane from the same coal. It is a fundamental limitation that we believe will always be the case. It is probably true for liquid hydrocarbons also. I say "probably" because we really haven't seen detailed comparative studies.

All the time we have ample supplies of coal, shale and biomass, we believe it is better to make methane or SNG than hydrogen for general use, because we have a system out there that is compatible with methane, burns methane and needs more methane, if it can get it. However, there are three applications that could justify making hydrogen from coal today. These are urban automobiles because of the clean burning characteristics of hydrogen; aircraft, because of the light weight of hydrogen; and as a chemical feedstock because of the chemistry.

The long-range application of hydrogen means that industry is unlikely to fund hydrogen development significantly today and yet R. & D. should be maintained because in the long run we won't have enough carbon to go around and we are going to have to change to something like hydrogen. Therefore, we should keep the research program alive, and it appears to be the Government's responsibility to provide the funding at this time.

The natural gas industry—I really can't speak for the industry as a whole, but my personal interpretation of their position is that the industry looks at hydrogen as a long-range way of staying in business in the nuclear and solar age. They have been supporting hydrogen research since 1971 and it is now supported through the Gas Research Institute, GRI. GRI is changing its attitude toward research in hydrogen at the present time.

It is replacing the applied projects on electrolysis and thermochemical hydrogen with a long-range and more basic program in hydrogen production at about the same funding level as before. But they are changing to a longer range fundamental program because they believe that hydrogen will not be required by the gas industry for 20 to 40 years.

The National Research Council Committee which met during 1978 and early 1979 was, I believe, an objective committee. It was drawn largely from outside the community of hydrogen specialists. I was on that committee, only one of three people who had perhaps a biased sort of enthusiasm toward hydrogen. I think their findings are representative of people largely looking in from the outside. Their conclusions were that in the near term, synthetic hydrocarbons will compete nicely with electricity and so we will have electricity and hydrocarbons as our main energy delivery systems. In the long term we will require expansion of nuclear, solar and coal resources, but they could not see that unlimited supplies of coal would always be available. They felt that hydrogen could be competitive with electricity in spite of the higher production cost, because of the better transmission, distribution and storage economics and the better economics of the conversion of the end-use equipment. They said "it would be prudent to have R. & D. results available within a decade to allow early implementing decisions on hydrogen to be made."

They recommended "there should be an R. & D. program which would address those constraints which would prevent hydrogen entering the economy today," and which would address production, transmission, storage and automobile use, incorporating wide-range and fairly broad, long-range programs. This program should go through the lab demonstration phase but not into large scale systems demonstrations.

In my opinion, the basic issues of hydrogen are concerned with the efficiency and cost of its production. Most of the other concerns that we have had have been adequately answered. We need comparisons of total systems all the way through from raw energy to end use. For example, we need to know if you start with coal what the end-use cost of hydrogen is versus SNG or gasoline or methanol.

I have not seen extensive studies done starting with the same ground rules, so we can compare apples with apples. If you start with nuclear and solar energy, we need more comprehensive comparisons of the cost and efficiency of end-use delivery of hydrogen versus electricity.

Finally, I firmly believe this is an area that requires Government support, because industry will not get fully behind a program which won't mature until beyond the year 2000.

Thank you.

[The prepared statement of Dr. Gregory follows:]

INSTITUTE OF GAS TECHNOLOGY

HYDROGEN AS A FUTURE FUEL

by

Derek P. Gregory

Testimony Submitted to

U.S. HOUSE OF REPRESENTATIVES
COMMITTEE ON SCIENCE AND TECHNOLOGY
Subcommittee on Energy Research and Production
Subcommittee on Energy Development and Applications

Washington, D. C.

June 25, 1980

IGT
EDUCATION RESEARCH

3424 SOUTH STATE STREET
IIT CENTER
CHICAGO, ILLINOIS 60616
AFFILIATED WITH ILLINOIS INSTITUTE OF TECHNOLOGY

HYDROGEN AS A FUTURE FUEL

Derek P. Gregory

1. Background and Introduction

I submitted testimony, backed up with supporting documents, to this committee on June 12, 1975. In that testimony, I outlined the potential role of hydrogen as a means of storing and delivering energy. Today, I would like to briefly recapitulate the reasons for considering hydrogen energy; indicate some recent technological and institutional changes that modify the urgency for the introduction of hydrogen; outline the position taken by IGT and the attitude of the gas industry and the National Research Council's committee on hydrogen; and state my personal recommendations for continued government support of research and development in this area.

2. Why Hydrogen?

When conventional fossil fuels become less available to the United States and the rest of the world, these countries must rely more on "renewables" such as solar and nuclear energy. But, unless these energy forms can be harnessed at the point of end use, a means of storage and delivery to the user is needed. Thus we have two choices: to develop an "all-electric economy" or to learn how to produce from the "renewables" a transportable fuel compatible with today's petroleum and coal-based fuels.

Transporting oil and gas in pipelines and underground delivery systems is recognized to be both less expensive and more efficient than transporting electric power. Also, the storage of these conventional "fuels" is easier and less expensive than storage of electricity. Thus, the search for a synthetic replacement "fuel" produced from nuclear or solar energy has merit.

Producing a synthetic hydrocarbon, resembling oil or natural gas, re- quires an abundant supply of hydrogen and carbon. Abundant hydrogen exists in a fully combusted or "burned up" state as water. The availability of abundant carbon is a different matter; abundant carbon found as coal or pe- troleum would no longer be available when fossil-fuels are more scarce, and carbon existing as CO_2 in the atmosphere or in limestone rocks is so diluted,

or so strongly chemically bound, that its separation requires large amounts
of energy that could never be recovered. Therefore, hydrogen itself, rather
than synthetic hydrocarbon, has received major attention.

It is possible to reverse the natural combustion process of hydrogen and
oxygen (from the air) to decompose water to hydrogen and oxygen. However,
in principle, this water-splitting reaction requires at least as much source
energy as that released when the hydrogen fuel is burned, and in practice,
it will require two or three times as much. Yet because hydrogen gas can,
in principle, be handled in the same way and by the same equipment now used
to move and store natural gas, it could become a replacement for natural
gas. The overall efficiency of converting nuclear or solar energy to useful
energy at the end-user's equipment through hydrogen production, transmission,
and combustion is not likely to be greater than that achieved through electricity production, transmission, and use. However, the economics of its
transmission, its ability to store, its ability to "package" on board a moving
vehicle, and above all, its ability to make use of existing distribution
and utilization equipment, make hydrogen an attractive alternative to electricity as a carrier of energy.

Hydrogen is not a source of energy, any more than an electric current
is a source. Hydrogen requires energy for its production, or generation, and
releases some of that energy on combustion. Thus, hydrogen is a future
carrier of energy, or a "fuel," not an energy source. It will not solve the
energy supply problem, but it will assist in the utilization of nuclear and
solar energy by addressing the energy delivery problem.

3. Recent Developments in Hydrogen Technology

Significant advances have been made at the hardware stage of the electrolytic production of hydrogen from water. Considerable progress has been made
at the laboratory level in developing "thermochemical" processes to split
water using heat rather than electricity. Two processes have been operated
continuously (using electric heaters); many others have been demonstrated to
operate on a batchwise scale, with the promise of achieving overall efficiencies
of 40% to 50%. It is too early to accurately forecast the costs of thermochemical hydrogen production. Encouraging results have been obtained by a

number of researchers on producing hydrogen from water by using direct sunlight, and by using processes resembling fermentation. These early results
show that there are other, potentially simpler paths for the production of
hydrogen, but they do not yet meet cost or performance criteria.

In tests limited to a 6-month duration, hydrogen gas has been shown to
be compatible with natural gas distribution equipment, though some meters
would have to be replaced with larger sizes. There are some unanswered questions as to the safety of welds if high-pressure gas-transmission lines were
operated on hydrogen, but operation in a safe mode does appear feasible. The
cost of long-distance energy transmission by hydrogen appears to be at least
one-third to one-tenth that of electricity. It appears quite possible to
store vast quantities of energy as hydrogen in underground formations, although the cost will be three or four times that of storing natural gas.
Hydrogen has been found to be interchangeable, or fully mixable, with natural
gas up to about 15% by volume, but beyond that, appliance burners will have
to be replaced or adjusted. So far, no insurmountable technical obstacles
to using hydrogen as a replacement for natural gas have been found.

4. Recent Changes in Energy Availability that Affect the Need for Hydrogen

The original enthusiasm for the so-called "Hydrogen Economy" that abounded
from 1972 to 1976 was as an alternative to the "Electric Economy" predicted
by many long-range energy planners. At that time, indications showed that
the natural gas supply was rapidly depleting, closely followed by oil, and
that the nuclear industry was greatly expanding. Hydrogen, as the "fuel
of the future," was believed to be capable of being, along with electricity, a
means of delivering nuclear energy. The events of the mid-70's have changed
this scenario. Conservation has decreased, at least temporarily, the demand
for energy, and increased exploration and R&D activities have promised the
availability of vastly increased amounts of natural gas, including that from
"unconventional sources." In parallel, R&D activities in hydrogen production
have shown that the cost of hydrogen from nuclear energy is not likely to be
less than $6.00 to $10.00 per 10^6 Btu (in today's dollars), while there should
be huge amounts of unconventional and substitute natural gas available (from
coal, shale, and biomass) significantly below these prices. Thus, the urgency
for developing a nuclear-based "hydrogen economy" has diminished.

On the other hand, the need for and availability of solar energy has
become more important in recent years. Much of the earlier thinking on using
hydrogen to store and carry nuclear energy can be applied to solar energy.
The cyclic nature of solar energy makes storage even more important, and the
concept of producing hydrogen from concentrated solar energy in central plants
becomes attractive. Again, the competitive cost of substitute and unconventional natural gas makes the time-scale for introduction of hydrogen fairly
distant and hard to pinpoint.

All this is not to say that hydrogen should be put "on the back burner"
for 50 years. Energy supply and availability scenarios can change drastically
and rapidly, as they did in 1973; an urgent switch to non-fossil energy sources
could someday be necessary. Hydrogen is the simplest chemical fuel that can
be produced from the combination of nuclear or solar energy with a raw feedstock available in unlimited abundance, and it is the only non-fossil chemical
fuel that is light enough to be considered for use in aircraft.

5.   The Position of IGT

Because no major obstacles have been found in the ultimate replacement of
natural gas by hydrogen, IGT believes that hydrogen should be regarded as a
long-term "insurance policy" by the gas industry, which will enable it to
continue to play a role in the nuclear/solar era. From a national point of
view, retaining and using much of the existing gas transmission, storage,
distribution, and utilization equipment for the delivery of·solar and nuclear
energy should result in less expense than reinforcing the electric system,
and it should result in more economic service to customers in .the long run.

The major technical problems have to do with the direct production of
hydrogen from thermal energy derived from the solar or nuclear plant. Further
research and development should result in solutions that will improve both
cost and efficiency. The large-scale production of hydrogen from solar con-
centrators of the type normally considered for deployment as electrical
generators (i.e., the proposed Barstow, California, installation) is of para-
mount importance as a possible way to overcome the storage and remote collector
problems inherent in the electrical analog.

If hydrogen-production technology can be improved, the use of hydrogen as
an automobile fuel appears to be a very satisfactory alternative to electricity

hydrogen storage is probably lighter and more compact than most electric batteries. However, a hydrogen vehicle can only be refuelled at a special hydrogen filling station, whereas an electric vehicle can be plugged in almost
anywhere.

The production of hydrogen from coal is within the scope of current
technology, but it appears to IGT that it will always be more expensive and less efficient than the corresponding production of substitute
natural gas (SNG) or liquid hydrocarbons from the same coal source, on an
equal energy basis. Unless there is some overriding advantage to be obtained from using hydrogen rather than SNG or liquid hydrocarbons, there
seems little to justify the major transition from conventional fuels to
hydrogen. In other words, as long as we have ample supplies of fossil-based
petroleum, coal, or biomass, it would be better to synthesize hydrocarbons
than hydrogen. Three uses of hydrogen that might justify its production
from coal (rather than the production and use of conventional fuels from
coal) are as an aircraft fuel (because of its light weight), as an urban
vehicle fuel (because of its cleaner burning characteristics), and as a
chemical feedstock (because of chemistry requirements).

IGT believes that, because it is so uncertain when hydrogen will be
introduced, industry will be reluctant to assume responsibility for R&D
funding. But because it is inevitable that we will ultimately need hydrogen,
R&D activities should continue at this time, and they should be mainly
underwritten by Government.

6. The Attitude of the Natural Gas Industry

The U.S. natural gas industry has supported and encouraged R&D on hydrogen
energy research since the year 1971. Hydrogen is recognized as a long-term
option, offering business an alternative to the sale of natural gas at some
future time. Hydrogen is an important intermediate in the conversion of coal
and shale to SNG, but it is not considered likely to emerge on its own as a
synthetic fuel for several decades. Mainly because of the reasons given in
Section 4, the Gas Research Institute has decided to end its applied research
program in hydrogen production from nuclear and solar heat and electricity
in 1980, and to substitute a broader, long-term program in more basic and
fundamental science relating to the production of hydrogen from water using
non-fossil energy sources.

GRI believes that the deployment of hydrogen as a replacement for methane will not be required for another 40 to 50 years. Thus there is ample time for a long-term research program, and there is no need to plunge ahead now to develop technology that could be obsolete before it has even been demonstrated. Accordingly, GRI is taking a fresh approach to hydrogen. A program of fundamental research will be pursued to explore all avenues of hydrogen production. The objective is to develop processes based on less conventional chemistry than currently envisioned, with the possibility of higher efficiencies and more benign process materials. GRI also seeks technology for producing a better fuel gas than hydrogen from renewable energy sources, for example, thermochemical methane. The gas industry also looks forward to the production of methane from biomass as a means of extending gas supply by deployment of renewable resources.

7. The Position of the National Research Council Panel on Hydrogen

A 12-member panel on hydrogen was convened by the Committee on Advanced Energy Storage Systems of the Assembly of Engineering of the National Research Council in the year 1977, and it published its report in 1979. To preserve objectivity, only three members of the panel had previous direct involvement in hydrogen-energy programs; the findings of the panel can be considered the consensus of a team that was largely unbiased. The charge to the panel was not specifically to express opinions about the merits or otherwise of hydrogen, nor recommend a research program, but to provide DOE with criteria for establishing the path, timing, and technical content of federal R&D programs on hydrogen. Nevertheless, the panel's conclusions and recommendations do indeed address the merits of hydrogen and make some specific program recommendations.

The panel thought that as long as fossil-fuel sources remain available at reasonable costs, natural or synthetic hydrocarbons will continue to compete with electricity as preferred energy carriers, but that in the long term, it will become necessary to expand nuclear, solar, and coal resources. And because they could not assume that unlimited supplies of coal will be available in the future for a variety of institutional and environmental reasons, they saw that nuclear or solar, as heat or electricity, would become the alternate sources. The panel felt that hydrogen might be competitive to electricity as an energy carrier, in spite of its higher production cost, because of its more economical transmission, distribution, and storage costs, and because it is easier to convert end-use equipment for hydrogen than to replace it with electric devices. Thus, the panel stated that it would be prudent to have R&D results on hand "within a decade" to enable early implementing decisions relating to the future role of hydrogen to be made. The panel recommended a well-conceived R&D program to consider some of the basic problems that constrain hydrogen's entrance into the economy. This program should give priority to reducing production costs, include transmission and storage concepts, include hydrogen-fuel-cell vehicle research, and provide a national data base. Such a program should be taken through the laboratory demonstration phase, even if near-term market needs cannot be identified, but should stop short of large-scale systems demonstration activities.

8. Recommendations

My personal recommendations are much in line with those of the National Research Council's panel. Because of the long-term nature of the need for hydrogen, it will be hard for industry to justify financial support of research programs, but the topic is important enough to warrant federally supported R&D. What is needed at this time is enough evidence to permit long-range planners to rely on the hydrogen option as being technically valid, and enough economic data to allow them to decide the proper time to implement hydrogen. For this, we need further improvements in hydrogen production technology from thermal and solar-radiation sources; further reassurance about the safety of hydrogen in storage and transmission systems; further development of solar-hydrogen-storage systems; and a better approximation of the ultimate cost of hydrogen delivered to the end-user on demand, compared to the equivalent cost of electricity.

In summary, although hydrogen energy may be considered by many as an idea whose time has not yet come, we must be ready to recognize when its time does arrive, and then rapidly bring about its implementation. The analogy to life insurance is a good one: It is an investment that will inevitably provide a benefit, but at an unknown time in the future, and to someone other than the original investor.

DEREK P. GREGORY, Vice President, Engineering Research

Dr. Gregory is Vice President of the Engineering Research Division of IGT. He is responsible for IGT's research programs in industrial and residential energy conservation, energy conversion and storage, energy systems analysis, alternative fuels production and utilization, and solar energy utilization. These programs include work on fuel cells, thermal storage, production and use of hydrogen and methane, industrial furnace development, residential appliance improvements, techno-economic evaluation of new energy technology, and energy supply and demand models.

Before joining the staff of IGT in 1970, Dr. Gregory was Research Manager at Energy Conversion Ltd., in England, where he directed research and development efforts on fuel cells and novel battery systems. From 1962 to 1966, Dr. Gregory was a project engineer at Pratt & Whitney Aircraft Division of the United Aircraft Corporation in East Hartford, Connecticut. He was responsible for the planning and coordination of electrochemical and physical research on all types of fuel cell systems.

Dr. Gregory received a B.S.c and a Ph.D. in physical chemistry from Southampton University, England.

Dr. Gregory has served, or is currently serving, on a number of task forces and working committees of the National Research Council, the Federal Power Commission and ERDA.

IGT

▶ A Center for Energy Technology

Founded in 1941, the Institute of Gas Technology is a worldwide independent, not-for-profit energy center Its main functions are

- -research and development performed under contract to industrial and government organizations,
- -educational programs and services, and
- -energy information and technology transfer services

IGT's R&D programs, currently funded at about $30 million, account for more than 90% of total activities Many of the major R&D projects and areas of activity at IGT are discussed in this document, including

- -IGT processes to produce liquids SNG and fuel gas from coal
- -liquids from Eastern U S oil shale,
- -fuel cells,
- -solar energy,
- -conservation and combustion,
- -residential space heating, and
- -unconventional gas

Other services include energy-related programs of research economics planning and education for industry and government

Staff

IGT's staff numbers more than 600 about half hold professional degrees of whom about half hold advanced degrees Consultants and other professional personnel are used on a part-time basis to complement IGT expertise and accommodate rapid growth without disruption of work in progress Of the total IGT staff, more than 60% are engaged in process and engineering research, about 25% in research and education, and the balance in support operations

Facilities

IGT's laboratories, offices, a computer center, library, and classrooms occupy 200,000 square feet of space in three IGT buildings on the campus of the Illinois Institute of Technology in Chicago Complete digital computer facilities, including computer-driven plotting capability, are available for the exclusive use of the staff The IGT library, one of the foremost energy librar-

⟶

Government-owned $30 million gasification research facilities at IGT in Chicago

IGT CENTRAL (ROOM 428-B)
-3424 SOUTH STATE STREET-
CHICAGO ILLINOIS 60616

IGT – *A Center for Energy Technology*

ies in the world is readily supplemented by computer searches of massive outside collections, and by the million-volume John Crerar Library, one of the premier technical libraries in the United States located adjacent to IGT The rapid availability of material and instant search capability are major factors in successful assessment and rapid completion of work in progress

At the 155-acre IGT pilot plant facility located about 15 minutes from the campus IGT conducts large-scale process development work including study of fluidization phenomena production of hydrogen from coal pipeline gas from coal industrial fuel gas from coal· pipeline gas and fuel oil from peat and oil shale and also performs analyses using large industrial combustion equipment Many of the large reactors available for research at the pilot plant facility are — like numerous other IGT facilities — unique, all offer sponsors the opportunity for a fast start and economical conduct of their research and development work

Research Scope

IGT conducts research in essentially all energy forms and is specifically involved in all fossil-fueled systems, including peat, petroleum fractions, as well as hydrogen and other nonfossil fueled systems, solar energy fuel cells ocean thermal gradients geothermal energy, wind, and biomass

systems Activities range from basic research through applied engineering and process design, and include the operation of large pilot plant facilities and the forming of consortia to develop demonstration and commercial plants, and, thereby, commercialize new processes

Other research services of IGT include chemical testing and analytical and instrument laboratories Resulting from long experience in sophisticated chemical research, IGT's technical laboratory skill has contributed to the development of several ASTM standards utilized in hydrocarbons research Moreover, IGT has made significant improvements in the analysis of low-sulfur light petroleum distillates by lowering the sensitivities of the methods for sulfur determination from the published value of 5 ppm sulfur to 0 1 ppm sulfur

The chemical research facilities have an extensive inventory of modern analytical equipment required to support IGT's staff and client requirements

Independent R&D

In addition to the various organizational research units, extensive independent research programs at IGT are directed toward better understanding of the behavior of fossil and nonfossil fuels and their interactions with the environment These programs utilize personnel from throughout IGT and are under the

supervision of senior IGT staff Major areas of study include reaction kinetics, heat transfer, thermodynamic and physical properties of gases fluid flow, catalysis, surface chemistry, molecular physics, electrochemistry, and microbiology Specific projects range from studies of new processes for the conversion of coal, biomass, sewage urban refuse and agricultural residues into clean, gaseous and liquid fuels to the computer modeling of energy supply and pricing systems

Education Services

Through its educational affiliation with IIT, IGT operates the school's Department of Gas Engineering IGT also conducts industrial short courses and conferences, and provides customized education services

Members

IGT's operations are guided by its Board of Trustees which is elected by Member companies, numbering about 200 Another affiliated group is International Associates who receive regular information services from IGT

GDC

In 1964, IGT organized Gas Developments Corporation as a wholly-owned taxpaying subsidiary to conduct domestic and international energy consulting services international education programs, and engage in commercialization of new technology ∎

Mr. OTTINGER. How much money is GRI devoting to this per year?

Dr. GREGORY. It was about $900,000 in applied hydrogen research. This year it is down to about $250,000 and next year it is scheduled to go back, I believe, to $1 million in basic research. So they are picking up the funding level they had last year.

Mr. OTTINGER. You said they are shifting away from applied hydrogen research.

Dr. GREGORY. They are closing down what they called their supply program on hydrogen but they've earmarked $1 million of their basic research program to work on hydrogen production technology.

Mr. OTTINGER. Where are they concentrating their research, do you know?

Dr. GREGORY. At the present time it is concentrated on thermochemical hydrogen production. In the future I think—and this is a conjecture, because I am not associated with GRI—I expect it to be concentrated on photochemical and biological production techniques, perhaps those longer range less certain technologies that we have already heard about at these hearings.

Mr. OTTINGER. What do you think the Government's involvement would be? Do you have any level of effort idea?

Mr. GREGORY. If we are looking at hydrogen as a fuel gas for natural gas replacement, that is long term and so there is no need for any major crash program. I would like to feel there is a little more funding than is available today, but certainly not more than double. It should be continued at at least its present level.

Mr. OTTINGER. You don't think it has any fairly near term application as an automobile fuel where it would be very important to the national interest?

Dr. GREGORY. I believe we need more systems studies and more economic studies of the comparison of making hydrogen from coal and delivering it for use in automobiles compared to making liquid hydrocarbons or methanol from coal and delivering it and using it in automobiles. I have not seen those comparative studies done on terms where we really feel we have a proper comparison.

If it should turn out that hydrogen is significantly better to the end user than a synthetic gasoline car, then we would require a lot of money for crash programs.

Mr. OTTINGER. I would think that is something we really ought to pursue.

Let us go to Dr. Mezzina.

STATEMENT OF DR. AL MEZZINA

Dr. MEZZINA. Mr. Chairman, thank you for inviting me and for offering me the opportunity and privilege of addressing this body. The testimony I will be presenting—and hopefully I will stay within my 10 minutes, Dr. Gregory—will be focused on the activities at Brookhaven. We will be talking about the background and rationale for the program as viewed from the BNL perspective. We will give you an overview of our activities and describe the directions which may be taken from programmatic actions.

It would be a good idea for me to read from the statement because I have a tendency to ramble if left on my own. Brookhaven National

Laboratory has provided technical and management support to the Department of Energy, Division of Energy Storage, since 1975. Early efforts in hydrogen energy storage systems aimed toward utility loan leveling applications associated with the potential exercise of the nuclear power option in the United States. In this application, off-peak electricity would be used to electrolyze water to produce hydrogen. The hydrogen would then be stored to feed fuel cell systems during peak periods. Some utilities have considered the direct injection of hydrogen into the natural gas distribution network. In this manner, off-peak electricity would be converted to an energy credit to be drawn upon in time of need or emergency. The apparent deferral of the nuclear power option has led to a shift in emphasis to the longer term prospects of renewable resource conversion.

While recognizing the long-term thrust of the program, BNL attempts to identify nearer term technology spinoffs. Clearly, hydrogen's versatility as a chemical commodity as well as a clean and environmentally benign fuel supplement with an excellent energy carrying capability motivates its early introduction into the energy infrastructure. Unfortunately, costs associated with hydrogen production, storage and distribution, when compared to current available alternatives, are the primary deterrents to near-term technology transfer on a wide scale.

Base technology development at BNL addresses future cost-effective and energy-efficient linking of dispersed renewable resources to end-use energy consumption centers. Abundant fossil fuel resources such as coal can be considered for conversion to hydrogen; but this must be weighed against other available options such as coal conversion to synthetic hydrocarbons. Conceivably, coal-derived hydrogen could be transported and distributed via the existing natural gas distribution network as a fuel supplement. Energy markets such as fuel cells could be reached and possible new markets in the commercial/industrial, and even the transportation sector, could be developed. Barriers and incentives of associated technical, economic, institutional and legal factors must be evaluated in developing the rationale for the natural gas supplementation option.

As far as the activities that are ongoing at Brookhaven, the areas of investigation pursued at BNL, through subcontract and in-house efforts are divided into four functional elements:

1. Electrochemical systems;
2. Storage systems and materials;
3. Chemical heat pumps; and
4. End-use applications and systems studies.

Consistent with the purpose of this hearing, discussion is limited to program elements dealing with hydrogen technology, which means I will not discuss chemical heat pumps.

In electrochemical systems, engineering development of solid polymer electrolyte water electrolysis systems maintains the highest programmatic and budget priority. Base technology advances have been applied to the designs and fabrication of low-cost high-efficiency test modules and systems. A 200 kilowatt system is now in the engineering development test phase. Verification of system cost and performance benefits will permit scaleup to large multimegawatt systems. Comparatively modest efforts in advanced alkaline systems have been pursued by testing improved electrodes and materials in a suitable test rig. These improvements are being equated to cost and will be used as a baseline comparison for other advanced water electrolysis systems being developed.

Insofar as storage systems and materials, metal hydrides have been identified as safe and effective storage materials for hydrogen, suitable for incorporation into systems as required, over a wide range of energy storage applications. However, again, evaluation of current materials available for near-term applications show that bulk hydride hydrogen storage is not practical, in general, because of the high cost. This would answer the question regarding the ammonia versus the metal hydrides shipment option, much heavier, a lot more volume and a lot more expensive.

Metal hydrides appear in a much more favorable light when viewed as short-term storage media operated in a rapid cycling mode. Mobile storage systems, compressors, separation/purification systems, and chemical heat pumps surface as potentially economically attractive systems development objectives.

Metal hydrides may assume a new resource recovery role resulting from technology spinoff from earlier investigations into metal hydrides poisoning mechanisms and high capacity storage materials. The resource derives from industrial process of gases and refinery gas which contain 12 to 60 percent hydrogen mixed with methane and various contaminants such as carbon monoxide, hydrogen sulfide and ammonia.

In 1978, this valuable commodity in refineries was used as fuel or flared in amounts estimated as in excess of 0.1 quad. Process cost projections indicate that hydrogen can be recovered at $1.25 per million Btu. This compares rather favorably to the current prices for hydrogen from steam reforming of natural gas which are as low as $6 per million Btu.

A new material for hydrogen storage systems (commercially available as a plastic filler) promises to take on the role of hydrogen bulk storage and transport media. The material is in the form of hollow glass microspheres, approximately 40 microns, that can be filled to pressures up to 6,000. To help you get a feel for this, if you knew you had to store hydrogen at 6,000 pounds per square inch, you would need a containment vessel of substantial thickness. The microspheres would allow you to carry that hydrogen in a paper bag even though pressurized to 6,000 pounds per square inch. Preliminary characterization of these materials verifies their potential for hydrogen storage with more than double the weight fraction of hydrogen stored compared to hydrides.

Efforts to determine the viability of underground storage of hydrogen have been completed—this, by the way, was done at the Institute of Gas Technology—and the results are positive from a technical and engineering standpoint with some cost constraints due in large part to the cost of hydrogen, per se.

So far as end-use applications and systems studies, small hydropower has been identified as an early candidate for renewable resource conversion demonstration. Indications are that small hydropower sites can be restored or developed to produce hydrogen consistent with local merchant hydrogen market requirements. Procurement actions have been completed for a cooperative project among DOE Division of Energy Storage and Hydroelectric Resource Development with New York State Energy Research and Development Authority and the city of Potsdam, N.Y.

The future activities and planning that is going on at Brookhaven National Laboratory is conducted under DOE policy guidance and budgetary constraints and recognizes that basic technology and systems development should be driven by user and market needs. Insofar as the Federal role, we feel that support to industry should be provided in those areas which promise substantial public benefit but are of high risk with long-term returns on investment. Future activities an programatic courses of action will seek to comply with criteria associated with markets identification and potential penetration of those markets. These criteria include:

Relevance to the technological base under development;

Potential for substantive impact within the near to midterm timeframe; and

Integration potential with the existing energy infrastructure.

Consistent with these criteria, the markets to be addressed include:

Chemical feedstocks via electrolytic hydrogen production;

Energy conservation in the residential/commercial/industrial sectors via chemical storage, chemical separation, and the chemical heat pumps;

In the longer term, transportation where we will attempt to tie mobile storage systems to efficient energy conversion systems such as fuel cells; and

Natural gas supplementation as the means for transporting and distributing hydrogen within distribution systems now in place.

That concludes my statement.

[The prepared statement of Dr. Mezzina follows:]

Statement by Mr. A. Mezzina, Program Manager, Chemical/Hydrogen Energy
Storage Systems Program, Brookhaven National Laboratory, at the Joint Hearing of
the House Science and Technology Committee, June 25, 1980.

HYDROGEN TECHNOLOGY DEVELOPMENT AT BNL

1.0 INTRODUCTION

Brookhaven National Laboratory has provided technical and management support to the Department of Energy, Division of Energy Storage, since 1975. Early
efforts in Hydrogen Energy Storage Systems aimed toward utility load leveling
applications associated with the potential exercise of the nuclear power option
in the United States. In this application, off-peak electricity would be used
to electrolyze water to produce hydrogen. The hydrogen would then be stored to
feed fuel cell systems during peak periods. Some utilities have considered the
direct injection of hydrogen into the natural gas distribution network. In this
manner, off-peak electricity would be converted to an energy credit to be drawn
upon in time of need or emergency. The apparent deferral of the nuclear power
option has led to a shift in emphasis to the longer term prospects of renewable
resource conversion.

While recognizing the long-term thrust of the program, BNL attempts to
identify nearer-term technology spin-offs. Clearly, hydrogen's versatility as a
chemical commodity as well as a clean and environmentally benign fuel supplement
with excellent energy carrying capability motivates its early introduction into
the energy infrastructure. Costs associated with hydrogen production, storage
and distribution, when compared to currently available alternatives, are the
primary deterrents to near-term technology transfer on a wide scale.

Base technology development at BNL addresses future cost-effective and
energy-efficient linking of dispersed renewable resources to end-use energy consumption centers. Abundant fossil fuel resources such as coal can be considered
for conversion to hydrogen; but this must be weighed against other available
options such as coal conversion to synthetic hydrocarbons. Conceivably, coal-
derived hydrogen could be transported and distributed via the existing natural
gas distribution network as a fuel supplement. Energy markets such as fuel

cells could be reached and possible new markets in the commercial/industrial, and even the transportation sector, could be developed. Barriers and incentives of associated technical, economic, institutional and legal factors must be evaluated in developing the rationale for the natural gas supplementation option.

2.0 BNL PROGRAM OVERVIEW

The areas of investigation pursued at BNL, through subcontract and in-house efforts, are divided into four functional elements: (1) Electrochemical Systems; (2) Storage Systems and Materials; (3) Chemical Heat Pumps; (4) End-Use Applications and Systems Studies. Consistent with the purpose of this hearing, discussion is limited to program elements dealing with hydrogen technology.

2.1 Electrochemical Systems

Engineering Development of solid polymer electrolyte (SPE) water electrolysis systems maintains the highest programmatic and budget priority. Base technology advances have been applied to the designs and fabrication of low-cost high-efficiency test modules and systems. A 200 kW system is now in the engineering development test phase. Verification of system cost and performance benefits will permit scale-up to large multi-megawatt systems. Comparatively modest efforts in advanced alkaline systems have been pursued by testing improved electrodes and materials in a suitable test rig. These improvements are being equated to cost and will be used as baseline comparison for other advanced water electrolysis systems being developed.

2.2 Storage Systems and Materials

Metal hydrides have been identified as safe and effective storage materials for hydrogen, suitable for incorporation into systems as required, over a wide range of energy storage applications. Evaluation of current materials available for near-term applications show that bulk hydride hydrogen storage is not practical, in general, because of the high cost. Metal hydrides appear in a much more favorable light when viewed as short-term storage media operated in a rapid cycling mode. Mobile storage systems, compressors, separation/purification systems, and chemical heat pumps surface as potentially economically attractive systems development objectives.

Metal hydrides may assume a new resource recovery role resulting from technology spin-off fron earlier investigations into metal hydrides poisoning mechanisms and high capacity storage materials. The resource derives from industrial process off gases and refinery gas which contain 12-60% hydrogen mixed with methane and various contaminants such as CO, H_2S, and NH_3. In 1978, this valuable commodity in refineries was used as fuel or flared in amounts estimated as in excess of 0.1 Quad. Process cost projections indicate that hydrogen can be recovered at $1.25 per million Btu. Current prices for hydrogen are as low as $6/MBtu.

A new material for hydrogen storage systems (commercially available as a plastic filler) promises to take on the role of hydrogen bulk storage and transport media. The material is in the form of hollow glass microspheres (approximately 40 microns) that can be filled to pressures up to 6000 psi. Preliminary characterization of these materials verifies their potential for hydrogen storage with more than double the weight fraction of hydrogen stored compared to hydrides.

Efforts to determine the viability of underground storage of hydrogen have been completed and the results are positive from a technical and engineering standpoint with some cost constraints due in large part to the cost of hydrogen, per se.

2.3 End-Use Applications and Systems Studies

Small hydropower has been identified as an early candidate for renewable resource conversion demonstraton. Indications are that small hydropower sites can be restored or developed to produce hydrogen consistent with local merchant hydrogen market requirements. Procurement actions have been completed for a cooperative project among DOE Division of Energy Storage and Hydroelectric Resource Development with New York State Energy Research and Development Authority and the City of Potsdam, New York.

3.0 FUTURE ACTIVITIES

Planning at Brookhaven National Laboratory conducted under DOE policy guidance and budgetary constraints recognizes that base technology and systems development should be driven by user and market needs. Support to industry is provided in those areas which promise substantial public benefit but are of high risk with long-term returns on investment. Future activities and programmatic courses of action will seek to comply with criteria associated with markets identification and potential penetration of those markets. These criteria include:

- relevance to the technological base under development;
- potential for substantive impact within the near to midterm time frame;
- integration potential with the existing energy infrastructure.

Consistent with these criteria, the markets to be addressed include:

- chemical feedstocks via electrolytic hydrogen production;
- energy conservation in the residential/commercial/industrial sectors via chemical storage, chemical separation, and chemical heat pumps;
- transportation—tying mobile storage systems to efficient energy conversion systems; and
- natural gas supplementation as the means for transporting and distributing hydrogen within distribution systems now in place.

Mr. OTTINGER. Thank you very much. We will get Dr. Kane started anyway. And then we will have to break for a vote I think.

STATEMENT OF DR. JAMES KANE

Dr. KANE. I suppose every witness starts out by saying it's a pleasure to be here. I would like to add a special vehemence to my tone in saying that today. I'd like to express my gratitude and I believe I express it to every member on the scientific research committee for the outstanding efforts this committee made in support of basic research in yesterday's appropriations bill. That just took less than a minute, but it is very sincere.

During my 10-minute presentation, I had intended to make some observations on some of the points covered in your invitation letter and to describe very briefly the DOE's hydrogen program and to give some rough budget numbers. And I'm suffering from the problem of being the late speaker in a program, my prepared remarks are a shambles, so I'll only go through a few of the points quickly. Almost everything I intended to say has been said, but I will hit them for a certain point of emphasis.

I'd like to congratulate you on your use of the words "delivery medium." There's a wide misconception that hydrogen is a source of energy. I think that has been adequately dealt with today. It is not a source. It takes energy to produce hydrogen. The analogy with electricity which several speakers have made today is a good one.

In very general sense, hydrogen can be used to couple any energy source to any desired application. So the question is not so much, "Can it be done?" but "Is it sensible to do so?" "Is it technically sensible? Is it economically sensible? Is it wasteful of energy?" The DOE's main program on hydrogen is intended to look at these various coupling mechanisms; that is, how do you get from hydrogen to a use that society needs. And the focus of the program is really the following three questions:

Given a source of energy, how do you get that hydrogen?

After you've got it, how do you transport and store it?

And, finally, after you've transported it and stored it, how can you best use it to fulfill society's needs at the point of consumption?

Before going into those three "how" questions, which is really the way our program is configured, perhaps I should discuss first where you can get hydrogen. Very quickly, you know that hydrogen is never found free in nature to any extent. It is found in really three main sources. One of these is biomass. Nature has split water for us and put the hydrogen into biomass. The second large source of it is the fossil biomass; in other words, oil, natural gas, shale oil, and a bit of it in coal, particularly western coal. And, finally, hydrogen is found in water which is an enormous resource.

In all three of those, hydrogen is chemically bonded, but certainly the difficulty of freeing it from water is by far the greatest. It usually, in my opinion, doesn't make sense to extract hydrogen from biomass. It is possible. But it is easier to convert biomass to other fuels that are more convenient to use in our existing systems: Alcohol, hydrocarbon, and so forth.

There are programs in the DOE to do those various things. Second, most hydrogen today, as has been said, comes from natural gas. In my opinion, again, this isn't a sensible source for widespread application, perhaps for specialty application, but not for a widespread one. Nor is petroleum or oil shale a sensible source for widespread applications. In the first place, you pay an energy penalty to transform them into hydrogen. And, second, they often don't fit the existing systems after you've transformed them. So, I think you should look to those first two, biomass and fossil energy sources, with the exception of coal, as ones that you would only use in an unusual situation where you very badly want the hydrogen for unique application.

So, water will be our main source. This takes energy. Of course, we get most of the energy back when we use the hydrogen. Now, I would refer you to a handout entitled "Production of Hydrogen From Various Energy Sources." I listed here the sources I had left after I told you I didn't think it made sense to use biomass or fossil energy with the exception of coal.

Coal, fission, fusion, and geothermal, which in general are heat generators—there's some talk that we might be able to use the charged particles from fusion or neutrons—can be used to generate hydrogen. And, finally, solar. So, across the top of my chart are the three main sources we'll have to look to, if we are going to convert to a hydrogen economy.

You'll notice I've underlined one approach that is common to all three energy sources, and that's electrolysis. You can burn coal, generate electricity, electrolyze water. You can use any of the heat liberators—namely, fission, fusion, and geothermal—to generate electricity and electrolyze water. Finally, you can use solar energy to generate electricity and electrolyze water. So, electrolysis has been talked about enough today. I don't think I'll go into any details, unless to respond to questions.

The second mode that is common to all three sources is that you can liberate heat, or in the case of coal, burn it to generate heat, and thermally decompose water to produce hydrogen. Dr. Funk discussed this in some detail. Again, I won't go into that any further. In general, the water doesn't care where the electricity came from. It does care to some extent where the heat comes from in that certain temperature regions are much easier to match the thermal decomposition cycles than others. So it is a pretty glib statement to say that the water doesn't care where the heat came from, because it does sometimes. The cost of it will depend tremendously on the quality of the heat.

So what's left really on my chart is two other ways to liberate hydrogen—Dr. Funk said three ways, and I've discussed two; Dr. Lindsey pointed out a fourth—all of which are on my chart. I think we should spend a minute or two then on No. 3, under coal, which is to use coal as a chemical to liberate hydrogen from water.

Liberating hydrogen from coal is the first step in gasification and it's usually the first step in direct liquefaction. So the Department of Energy is spending a very large amount of money on the technology of generating hydrogen from coal. I don't plan to discuss that much either.

Being more of a scientist than an engineer, I'd say as a first approximation that whether you stop your process at hydrogen or whether you proceed on to methane or perhaps even methanol is going to be at the second level of cost. It won't make any factors of two changes. My opinion is that whether you stop with hydrogen or proceed on to the other fuels, it's going to be about a 10 percentage effect in cost. Don't quote me on that, but it's not going to be a dramatic difference in cost. Almost all the coal syntheses steps start with the generation of hydrogen. OK. On the bottom right, under solar, I used the word photon that is technically not too accurate. It serves to lump all the things Dr. Lindsey discussed under the one heading of solar energy production. Solar energy comes in little packages called photons. You don't have to degrade them down to heat to use them to split water and get hydrogen. There are ways we can use the energy of the photon directly and Dr. Lindsey very accurately went through the three possible ways.

If you distinguish carefully, they're using ways nature has worked out. She discussed the use of algae, which in general helps produce hydrogen. They are usually producing other things, but their processes can generate hydrogen on the way to what they are actually trying to produce. Some of them actually do produce hydrogen.

And so we can improve on nature perhaps by genetic engineering or see if we can get hydrogen by a way that nature has already done most of the work.

Second, as Dr. Lindsey pointed out, you can mimic nature and try to make systems that are artificial. If you want to call them in vitro, that's correct, but which mimic photosynthetic processes.

And, finally, we can use totally artificial processes, and she gave two examples, one where you use what the scientists call homogeneous or solution processes in which you put in certain chemicals to separate the charges. The photon comes in and splits these chemicals and deposits the negative charges precisely as the photon does in the photovoltaic cell which is made out of silicon. Then you can use this charge separation to do chemical reactions. And there have been questions on that. The other way is what we call heterogeneous processes, which just means there is a solid material which is usually a solid state photovoltaic-like material.

That's the end of my talk on production and you can see my program has aspects of every one of those and when I sum up I will go through the budget.

In transportation and storage—this has been very well covered— there can be problems particularly with more modern pipelines that have higher quality steel and are welded to perform at a higher fraction of their yield strength. These problems have to be looked at carefully, so it is probably not right to say there are no problems. There are problems, but I think they are manageable in using pipelines.

[The prepared statement of Dr. Kane follows:]

104

Statement of Dr. James S. Kane
Before the
House Science and Technology Subcommittees on
Energy Research and Production
and
Energy Development and Applications

June 25, 1980

I am pleased to have the opportunity today to testify on the subject of
"Hydrogen: Production and End Uses." There is a perception by some that
hydrogen is cheap and environmentally clean, and should be vigorously
promoted for various domestic energy uses. I will comment on several
aspects of that perception. Hydrogen has rightly received attention
in recent years as an energy delivery medium because of (1) its versatility
as an end use fuel, (2) the potential for its production from most primary
energy sources, (3) its ease of transport in the gaseous state, and (4)
its minimum environmental impact at the point at which it is used.

Hydrogen is used extensively in the industrialized world for the synthesis
of chemicals and in petroleum refining to increase gasoline fractions and
upgrade sour or sulfur bearing crudes. Petroleum refining uses about 50%
of the hydrogen consumed; fertilizer production consumes about 35%, principally for the production of anhydrous ammonia. Principal end uses of
the future are expected to be in synthetic fuels processing, chemicals, and
petroleum refining to a decreasing extent. Coals with high sulfur content,
like sour crudes, would be unusable without treating with hydrogen to remove
the sulfur as hydrogen sulfide. Other potential future applications include
hydrogen fuel cells to generate electricity, hydrogen fueled engines and
turbines for surface, air and space transportation, and possibly domestic
and industrial heating. These uses rely on the availability of relatively

inexpensive and abundant supply of energy from primary sources.

Approximately 75% of the hydrogen used today comes from natural gas with most of the rest coming from petroleum fractions. In anticipation of diminished supplies of natural gas and oil, other sources must be considered Hydrogen occurs in vast quantities in nature, but never as free hydrogen. It is invariably chemically bound, and energy is required to free it. Hydrogen is most easily available from green plants and from natural gas and oil, but the amounts are limited, and it is usually preferable to use these comparatively rare sources for other purposes. There are essentially limitless amounts of hydrogen in the earth's water, and it is to this source that we must turn for hydrogen if its use is to be widespread.

There are four principal pathways for obtaining hydrogen from water. Water can be dissociated, or "split," by heat. Water can be decomposed into hydrogen and oxygen by electricity, through a process called electrolysis. The oxygen in water can be removed by reacting it with carbon, from coal, for example, leaving hydrogen free. And water can be broken into hydrogen or its compounds by the energy in sunlight, by a variety of processes, many of which occur naturally.

It is therefore possible to obtain hydrogen from nearly any energy source. Using hydrogen as the energy carrier, it is also possible to connect these sources to the many end use apolications needed by society. This is not to say, however, that the coupling is necessarily economic, simple, or desirable. Each of the sources will have specific problems that must be

solved, as will each of the applications. The Department's hydrogen program consists mainly of research and development on what we believe to be
the most important of these problems.

In your letter of invitation you asked that I address questions related to
production, transmission and storage, and end use. You asked that I do
this in the context of technical, economic and environmental issues.

Production

I do not believe that natural gas, petroleum or oil shale should be widely
used as sources of hydrogen. The resources yield products that fit nicely
with our current use patterns, and they should be reserved for these uses,
with rare exception.

The widespread use of hydrogen therefore clearly implies massive energy
sources other than oil and gas: coal, nuclear fission, nuclear fusion,
geothermal and solar. There are major efforts in the DOE on each of
these; I will not describe them today. Our hydrogen research is not aimed
at the primary energy production process, but rather at how this energy
can be used to obtain hydrogen.

As previously mentioned, any source of electricity and many sources of
heat can be used to obtain hydrogen. The process of electrolysis is
quite mature technically; it is currently used industrially. There are
many opportunities to increase efficiency, however, and the DOE FY-79
expenditures on electrolysis research were $3.9 million. For example,
electrolysis using improved solid polymer electrolytes to increase efficiency and operability at higher pressures and temperatures will require
additional research.

The use of heat to "split" water is far less advanced technically; it is inherently a very sophisticated chemical process. In FY-79 the DOE spent $3.3 million in this area. Direct thermal dissociation would require very high temperatures (about 2300°C) and accordingly is dependent on the availability of abundant high temperature heat and materials suitable for high temperature duty. Indirect thermal hydrogen production is accomplished in two or more separate chemical reaction steps which have the overall effect of dissociating water to hydrogen and oxygen. This is sometimes referred to as a thermochemical cycle because all reactants other than water are returned eventually to their original chemical state; the only material consumed is water. The efficiency for converting thermal energy to hydrogen by thermochemical cycles has the potential of exceeding that of electrolytic conversion. However, the complexity of thermochemical cycles for such thermally efficient systems tends at present to offset that potential efficiency advantage.

Additional research is necessary to improve thermochemical dissociation. For example, evaluation of new cycles is often impossible because of inaccurate or non-existent thermochemical data.

There is no explicit DOE program to obtain hydrogen using coal. There is, however, a very major effort on coal gasification and indirect coal liquefaction. The results of this R&D are highly relevant to the production of hydrogen, if it should be decided that hydrogen is more desirable than coal-derived methane or liquid fuels.

The production of hydrogen by solar energy is a special case. Hydrogen-producing organisms that derive their energy from sunshine are found in nature; we are looking at ways to use and improve them. In addition, DOE has a vigorous research program aimed at photochemical hydrogen production. The research consists of examining processes by which water can be split into hydrogen and oxygen by the direct action of the solar photons, without first converting sunshine to electricity or heat. This research is currently at a very basic level, it is high risk, but it is also scientifically very exciting and I believe, very promising. I am personally very enthusiastic about its prospects. In 1979 we spent $7.8 million in this area. More research is needed on such topics as picosecond spectroscopy, porphyrin chemistry, photochemical mechanisms and kinetics, and photoinduced electron transfer in mixed organic-inorganic systems, for example.

Transportation and Storage

If hydrogen use is to be versatile and convenient, there must be means of transporting and storing it. Fortunately, much of the required technology exists.

The compatability of hydrogen in the current natural gas distribution pipelines has been the subject of study. Hydrogen requires higher standards of containment than does natural gas because of its comparatively small molecular size; it escapes rapidly through small cracks and holes. Many pipelines that are suitable for natural gas would not be suitable for hydrogen. Hydrogen also diffuses readily into many structural metals where it reacts to form hydrides which severely embrittle the material, with the potential of catastrophic failure. All components of hydrogen systems must be designed to prevent this embrittlement.

The storage of hydrogen is not as convenient as the liquid fuels we use now or expect to use in the future. Cryogenic storage requires specialized storage vessels and has, of course, an efficiency penalty. Liquifying hydrogen and storing it at low temperatures consumes energy. Large underground gas storage caverns appear possible for bulk storage, although the rate of escape through cracks would be greater than that of natural gas. Hydrogen can be stored by reacting it with certain metals to form hydrides; the hydrogen is released by heating. Hydride storage systems are, at present, very heavy and use costly materials. For example, an iron-titanium alloy vehicular storage tank, which would be sufficient for storing 200 equivalent miles of hydrogen, would weigh approximately 3300 pounds or over 40% of a moderate sized car equipped to handle the added weight. Lighter weight hydrides have at present other disadvantages such as requiring fuel consumption to remove the hydrogen. Research is needed to reduce weight, increase capacity, and of course, to reduce cost.

End Use

The technology is mostly available for converting hydrogen to needed applications at the point of use. The exception to this is the generation of electricity, where there is need for additional research on fuel cells. Fortunately, much of the research and development on hydrocarbon fuel cells being done in DOE is applicable also to hydrogen fuel cells. In fact, hydrogen is in general a preferable fuel cell fuel. Fuel cells, of course, have the additional advantage of providing very useful heat as a by-product.

The use of hydrogen as a fuel for heating is a known technology. It is often a preferred fuel for this purpose. It is non-toxic, odorless, and its combustion products can be extremely low in pollutants.

The use of hydrogen for vehicular travel is also largely within the capabilities of current technology. Automobile engines and aircraft turbine engines have been operated on hydrogen. In these applications it is often a highly desirable fuel, from both technical and environmental considerations

In sum, the use of hydrogen at the point of consumption appears to present no great obstacles, although specific problems are sure to arise. And its virtues of cleanliness, wide limits of combustion, clean combustion and high energy per pound often make it an extremely desirable fuel.

Safety and Environmental Issues

Although hydrogen is perceived by many to be especially dangerous, the technology exists to handle it safely. There are hazards with any flammable fuel. Other than its combustibility, hydrogen presents no unusual problems.

The end uses of hydrogen tend to be environmentally attractive. The main environmental question is sure to be that of the primary energy source. Since the production of hydrogen is likely to be at large, concentrated sources, the pollutants produced will also be concentrated, similar to those of electrical generating stations.

As can be seen from my presentation to this point, the most important question related to the use of hydrogen is not can we use it, but should we use it. It is probably technically possible to connect almost any energy

source to any energy use by means of hydrogen. What should govern our
decision on hydrogen use is therefore its costs, provided we include
in costs the appropriate environmental considerations.

With currently available sources of energy, there is little basis for
proceeding rapidly toward widespread hydrogen use. There are indeed
special situations where its use will be highly beneficial -- an operation where low pollutant emissions are crucial, such as underground mines -
is an example.

The future uses of hydrogen are less clear. In any event, its use will be
limited by the availability of sources of energy. In each situation, we
will have to examine all considerations, and decide for that case whether
hydrogen or some other energy carrier is best. The basis for choice will
be primarily economic.

My personal opinion is therefore that the current Department program is
appropriate. We are not "crashing" toward the widespread use of hydrogen,
but we are examining those areas where R&D will make hydrogen more economically competitive. I believe that the use of water-derived hydrogen will
increase as prices of currently available fuels rise. Likely areas of
growth are its use in the chemical industry and intercontinental jet aircraft, but this will not be in the next decade.

I believe that the Federal role as related to hydrogen should be similar to
that of other energy related technologies. This includes support of high
risk basic and applied research, evaluation and assessment of technological
options in the context of overall energy needs, and the preliminary
development of promising options to advance the timely entry of the
industrial sector.

Thank you.

DEPARTMENT OF ENERGY·

Expenditures on Hydrogen Research

| | ($ in millions) | |
PRODUCTION	FY-79	FY-80
Electrolysis	3.9	3.3
Thermal Decomposition of Water (Water "Splitting")	3.3	2.9
Solar Photochemical Production	7.8	8.8
Hydrogen from Coal	-	- *
Total Production	15.0	15.0
TRANSPORTATION AND STORAGE		
Hydride "Carrier" Research	4.2	3.7
Materials Problems Related to Hydrogen	4.4	4.0
Total Transportation and Storage	8.6	7.7
END USE		
Fuel Cells	-	- *
Vehicular Travel	0.1	0.1
Applications Related to Low Head Hydropower	0.5	0.4
Total End Use	0.6	0.5
TOTAL HYDROGEN PROGRAM	24.2	23.2

* Large effort in Fossil Energy Program. The results are highly relevant to hydrogen.

PRODUCTION OF HYDROGEN FROM VARIOUS ENERGY SOURCES

COAL

1. BURN, GENERATE ELECTRICITY, ELECTROLYZE WATER

2. BURN, GENERATE HEAT, THERMALLY DECOMPOSE WATER

3. REDUCE WATER TO HYDROGEN CHEMICALLY

(COAL ALSO CONTAINS SOME HYDROGEN)

FISSION, FUSION, GEOTHERMAL (HEAT GENERATORS)

1. GENERATE ELECTRICITY, ELECTROLYZE WATER

2. THERMALLY DECOMPOSE WATER

SOLAR

1. CONVERT SOLAR ENERGY TO ELECTRICITY, ELECTROLYZE WATER

2. CONVERT SOLAR ENERGY TO HEAT, THERMALLY DECOMPOSE WATER

3. DECOMPOSE WATER PHOTOCHEMICALLY (DIRECT SOLAR PRODUCTION)

TRANSPORTATION AND STORAGE OF HYDROGEN

- PIPELINES

- COMPRESSED GAS

- CRYOGENIC HYDROGEN

- CHEMICALLY BOUND IN METALS, OR IN OTHER COMPOUNDS SUCH AS AMMONIA

USE OF HYDROGEN AT POINT OF CONSUMPTION

- CHEMICAL SYNTHESIS

- HEAT – BURNERS

- WORK – ENGINES, TURBINES

- ELECTRICITY – FUEL CELLS

Mr. OTTINGER. How about plastic pipe?

Dr. KANE. I can assure you that there are no chemical problems. The idea of perhaps using a composite pipeline— has that been looked into?

Dr. GREGORY. We ran plastic pipes at low pressures, 50 pounds and below in the last 6 months with no obvious change, no serious leaks.

Dr. KANE. And I imagine that would apply certainly to composite reinforced pipelines. You could get the pressure higher, if you really wanted to.

Mr. OTTINGER. The exigencies of the House of Representatives require us to go vote. We will recess briefly and then resume and try to wrap up when we get back.

[Recess.]

Mr. OTTINGER. Sorry for the interruption, Dr. Kane. Why don't you pick up where you left off.

Dr. KANE. I will pick up on the transportation and storage part. I really don't have much more to say about the pipelines. Compressed gas is a known technology, and there are always in these known technologies new little wrinkles. I was very interested to hear Dr. Mezzina talk about putting in little microballoons. The microballoons, as he pointed out, are something you can buy in ton lots probably because they are used to reinforce plastic in industry. Cryogenic hydrogen, I also won't talk much about. There are certainly experts here in the audience who could answer questions. Certainly, NASA has put in a great deal of time and effort on the safe handling of large amounts of cryogenic hydrogen—at least in the systems NASA used. They accomplished it.

Finally, the chemically bound, or otherwise bound hydrogen, has been discussed today. These points that I put on my VuGraphs were meant to be places that I would point out to you where we were doing research. As Dr. Mezzina pointed out, we are doing a considerable amount of research in bonding hydrogen in metals where there are still opportunities to lower the weight of the system and to make the hydrogen more easily regenerated and, of course, lower the cost.

The final aspect of hydrogen, to my way of organizing it, is its use at the point of consumption. Here there is perhaps even less research going on. To use it in the form of chemical synthesis, as has been pointed out by several people today, is relatively straightforward and the industry exists. It is today consuming hydrogen.

And for heat, conversion of hydrogen to heat, burner technology, again, people have pointed out that often hydrogen is a preferred fuel because of its low emittance of pollutants at the point of consumption. It also has some other technical aspects which make it excellent. It has what scientists call wide limits of combustion. This means you can engineer the flame, sometimes in a desirable sort of way.

As far as turning hydrogen into work, there are always detailed questions, but there are no fundamental questions about using hydrogen to propel different kinds of vehicles, either through engines, turbines or even hypersonic ramjets, if you are talking about high altitude travel in the future.

The one aspect in which there is considerable opportunity for research, in my opinion, is converting hydrogen to electricity at the point of consumption. There, of course, it is done in a straight forward way by burning hydrogen and turning the heat into electricity. But certainly in many ways, the preferred way would be to use fuel cells at the point of consumption because, as you certainly know, they are more easily distributed and they have the virtue of releasing what to them is waste heat at a place where you can often use it for space heating and so on. So research on more efficient fuel cells certainly is an area of effort. Now I'll sum up, if it's all right with you, Mr. Chairman, and then go through the budget with just a very few comments on the DOE budget and then respond to your questions.

Mr. OTTINGER. I'd like to know where we are on the budget, and assuming there was no OMB and no Budget Committee in the House or Senate, what you would think the national program ought to look like for exploitation of hydrogen and with what speed it ought to be done and where do you think these uses come in.

Dr. KANE. I'll try to hit those points and if I don't do well, I'll expect your questions.

To sum up then, the major question is—all across hydrogen—and I think there's been great unanimity today amongst the witnesses, the question is not can. but should. we do it? Does it make sense? And the sense ultimately boils down to does it make economic sense.

If the technology can be improved, there are a number of areas where it will make more sense. But that is really always the question. It has been pointed up very nicely today in the testimony. Is it wise to convert coal to hydrogen rather than to, say, alcohol or synthetic fuels? In my opinion—I think I've answered that already—with very few exceptions, it does not. Because the system currently exists to handle liquid fuels, it would be cheaper—and that comes, believe me, from a basic scientist and not an economist or a good engineer, so——

Mr. OTTINGER. When we make these economic calculations, do we put in and should we not put in the penalty we pay for having to import oil to the extent that you can use hydrogen for substitution of existing oil uses? In my way of thinking we have $90 billion to play with. The thing can be $90 billion uneconomical and you can do it in this country and we still come out far ahead not having to spend that $90 billion for imported oil.

Dr. KANE. I certainly agree with you. I think the next question you ask how best can I spend it to displace those imports, and again your answer may come up a synfuel rather than hydrogen, if coal is the source. I'm not taking a question on that other than I feel very strongly that the economics will favor, except for a few unusual cases, which I will mention later—systems where the existing structure can handle it. Liquid fuels are a wonderful thing for our automotive vehicles. The system is there and in place. People have investments in automobiles that use those. The major use of hydrogen in the future will be limited by availability of the energy source and not by hydrogen technology.

Mr. OTTINGER. Let me cut in there a minute, because I've been told for a cost of something like $100 to $125 per vehicle you could use your existing automobile engine with hydrogen and that the conversion cost is relatively inexpensive; is that accurate?

Dr. KANE. I think there are others that can give you a better number. My response to that is the conversion to get the vehicle to burn the hydrogen should be relatively simple, but building it to carry enough hydrogen to make it practical I don't think is simple or cheap.

Mr. OTTINGER. Does anybody have any information?

Dr. MEZZINA. I can give you a feel for the problem. What you say is absolutely true that you can convert the vehicle to burn hydrogen, but the problem is not that. The problem is carrying the fuel.

Mr. OTTINGER. I'm told you can carry the fuel in hydrides.

Dr. MEZZINA. Sure you can, but if you wanted to carry the equivalent of 20 gallons of gasoline, I would venture a guess in terms of Btu's—will you help me, Jim—I think the weight would come out to be—with hydrides—on the order of 4,000 pounds.

You are also paying the penalty of carrying that additional weight with you. Now the other approach that one has is to find a much more efficient way of utilizing that hydrogen. For example, if Jim Kane had his way, and he invented an efficient low-cost fuel cell, we might have a fuel cell to be used for driving that automobile. We are still in the area of developing base technology. But insofar as having what we are used to today in terms of a vehicle that can operate at the appropriate speeds or velocities and ranges, et cetera, with currently available technology, I don't think we can do it. I have left out the question of cost.

Mr. OTTINGER. Something I don't know about is reliability. But they said you could convert not only the engine but also the car to be able to store hydrogen bromides I believe it was, without any tremendous weight problem. I'm not sure what the hydride was, but it was for about $100 to $125. That doesn't ring a bell with you?

Dr. GREGORY. There is a company out on the west coast that claims to be able to produce a liquid hydride very inexpensively. They will not indicate what it is and it is very hard to imagine what it could be—if they are right, I think they are talking about $300 to convert a vehicle. If you go with metal hydrides, you have to restrict the range of the vehicle just to make the concept make sense, but it is still lighter than an electric car. But I think you could probably convert a vehicle for a few hundred dollars, but the problem is where do you fill it up?

Mr. OTTINGER. If you decided it was economic, then presumably you would work out a distribution system through your existing service station. That is not difficult when you talk about the electric car. What is contemplated there, if the thing gets going, is that the existing service stations would store fully charged batteries and you would go in and just exchange the batteries. The distribution system exists and it could work just as well for hydrogen or charged batteries as it does for gasoline. It doesn't mean it is like snapping a finger, but it could be done.

Dr. KANE. I think the major use of hydrogen in the future is clearly going to be limited by the availability of the energy source. Anything I say, of course, is my own interpretation. Improvements in technology always help. I think that is a fair statement. The use of hydrogen is going to increase due to some of its unique properties. I can see specialized cases in which you may want an engine that runs without polluting the environment—the fact is that hydrogen is clean—such as underground mining, you would trade off electrical equipment for hydrogen. Planes, inspite of the fact that people have a tendency to laugh when you talk about hydrogen-burning airplanes, in my opinion, may be one of the first things we will see. The reason is the structure may be simpler. There's no question you can design an airplane that will burn hydrogen. There has been an airplane that has actually flown with one engine running on hydrogen.

It is, again, probably a preferable fuel in a technical sense. It does less harm to the turbine and it is a controllable fuel. In spite of the fact that hydrogen has a low energy density in terms of volume, volume is not usually a consideration in designing an aircraft. So it is possible that for international airplanes, the test case might be in the next 25 years or even sooner. There's nothing technically impossible about that at all. Purely, is it worthwhile doing it?

Dr. OTTINGER. It can be done safely?

Dr. KANE. The safety question always come up. There are a lot of people who have handled a lot of hydrogen safely, so the technology exists to handle hydrogen safely. There is a hazard to any combustible fuel. Hydrogen has to be handled correctly. It is probably less forgiving of mistakes. Occasionally, I have seen somebody with a cigarette in their mouth at a service station, and I cannot imagine at a hydrogen service station anybody with a cigarette in their mouth.

Mr. OTTINGER. Can the hydrogen fuel take an airplane crash without greater risk of an explosion?

Dr. KANE. The crash question is a technical question and you almost have to take each situation. Let me just give you a small taste of it and then I won't try to give you an answer on which is the more dangerous. Fuels like hydrogen—hydrogen has the wonderful virtue of diffusion. It dissipates very rapidly when it is freed. So it gets away from where it was. There's no pool of it that stays around and burns.

On the other hand, it has very low-flammability limits. There are some disadvantages. I think you would almost have to analyze very carefully the specific accident and say which would be worse, this or say liquified natural gas or gasoline. They all give off a lot of energy, and, if you handle them wrong, there are real problems. In spite of the *Hindenberg* effect, I'm not at all sure that a good system couldn't be devised to handle hydrogen safely. You start with airplanes that would have a relatively small number of people doing the handling. Hydrogen is more rigorously controlled in the way it is handled rather than distribute it to the general public. With regard to environmental considerations, I'll just make a general statement, because other witnesses have commented on it. It is usually very clean at the point of consumption, granted. Also, the energy has to come from somewhere. Somebody talked about the very large scale facilities that would be used to make hydrogen. There would be enormous concentrations of energy at the facilities and probably pollutants. So the glib remark that hydrogen is always clean has to be received with a great deal of skepticism. It may or may not be. Certainly at the point of consumption, there's a great deal to be said for it.

Finally, our program. We have a flexible program and the point of it is to try to look at these coupling points between the source of hydrogen and the ultimate use and see where research can have leverage on this system.

The last page of my formal written testimony contains a budget rundown as closely as I could bring it together of where we are spending money in hydrogen. Now I want to make it very clear we did not include the very large amount of money being spent by Fossil Energy related to the synthesis of hydrogen from coal, nor did we include in that the amount of money that the Office of Fossil Energy is spending on fuel cells. And I'd just like to make the point that much of the technology that is coming out of fossil energy programs to gasify and liquefy coal especially indirect liquefaction, is pertinent to the generation of hydrogen, should you decide to do so.

And, similarly, most of the room temperature fuel cells being worked on today actually perform better with hydrogen than they do with hydrocarbon fuels, so the work on them would be applicable to hydrogen problems. But those two were excluded in my budget summary. My budget summary really concerns the chemical aspects of production and some of the metallurgical aspects, the carrier research, the thermal water splitting, and some of the more shorter range.

The sum, as you can see, is roughly $24 million. I realize I've gone through this tremendously fast, but much of what I am intending to say has already been said, so I will respond to questions at this time.

Mr. OTTINGER. The main question I have is, If you had no constrictions on you, what kind of a hydrogen research program would you promote?

Dr. KANE. Let me break that into two parts, and I will give an answer to half. I will ask Dr. Swisher to answer the other half because he is really more acquainted with his part of the program than I am. I think Dr. Lindsey was correct that we could wisely spend a little more research on photo methods of production. I wouldn't agree with her that we could find enough skilled researchers to absorb a factor of two in that area. I don't feel a sense of urgency on the hydrogen question. I guess we could spend additional money. As I said previously, to me what will govern the use of hydrogen is not the technology represented in this budget. What will are the number of sources of energy, be they solar, some aspects of it, nuclear, or coal. Today the choices are very limited. And I've already told you I didn't think coal was a very wise way.

So I don't feel that much of an expansion is warranted. Sure I could find some areas to put it in. There has been some mention today, but not doubling by any sense of the word.

Mr. OTTINGER. Has the Department tried the same sort of effort, for instance, as we have done in photovoltaics, to identify specific goals and specific time periods, how to get from here to there?

Dr. KANE. Maybe Dr. Swisher can address that part of it. I think, in general, no. And let me tell you why I believe we haven't. In the case of photovoltaics there are some economies of scale plus some efficiency improvements that at least forecast in some people's minds, a really dramatic change in cost. I don't think you have heard anybody today, say they could double the efficiency of the electrolyzer, correct me if I am wrong. Those factors of two aren't there.

In the solar business there are probably really factors out there available and that's why you can plan on it. Again—maybe that's not a satisfactory answer—but we've never laid out the path from where we are today to, for instance, a much better electrolyzer simply because we don't think the enormous gain is there. We keep getting some good ideas as we support them, but, no—Dr. Swisher?

Mr. OTTINGER. Would it be useful for us to call together the people who are working in this field and try to arrive at that kind of a goal in this area?

Dr. KANE. I think it is always good to ask the workers in the field what possibilities they see for improvement and how far they think it might go and then you have to make a judgment to put the money there or someplace else. And I think the first thing you would have to do is call your group together and ask them what would be the possible goals you could obtain in economics and then make the judgment of whether that was worth it compared to putting the money someplace else.

Dr. SWISHER. I represent the more applied research and development program in hydrogen in the Department of Energy, and we do have program plans with very well defined goals on electrolytic hydrogen production, thermochemical hydrogen production, and hydrogen storage.

I, as a part of my responsibilities, have to compete the hydrogen activities against thermal storage and flywheels and a number of other things. During the last few years, in these times of fiscal constraints, there has been some problem in setting priorities. Some things with near term payoff are now being pushed faster at the expense of some others. We have cut back some on our hydrogen program. I am disappointed we had to do that.

Mr. OTTINGER. What did we lose in your opinion?

Dr. SWISHER. Well, for example, our budget in fiscal year 1979 in my program was $6.3 million. This year, fiscal year 1980, it is $4.5 million. The budget request for fiscal year 1981 is $2.5 million.

Mr. OTTINGER. What I am asking is what has the Nation lost with that loss of budget?

Dr. SWISHER. We are only able to work on what we think are pacing technology problems. We try to work on things that we think are the most difficult and leave the straightforward things go till later. Furthermore, we are not working on all of the difficult problems now, which means that we will have to try to do more later after some of the projects with near-term payoff are completed.

Mr. OTTINGER. Is it of a nature that you can calculate that this kind of cut would delay the use of hydrogen for any of these end uses by a given number of years? For example, you might have hydrogen available for automobiles or fuel cells or whatever in 1985 instead of in 1990, if you had the extra research money.

Dr. SWISHER. Well, we can make estimates. I think the pace of the hydrogen technology program now is about half what it was 2 years ago, which means that the time for having the technology on the shelf is going to be delayed by a factor of two.

Mr. MCCORMACK. Will the gentleman yield?

Mr. OTTINGER. I'm going to have to let you take over.

Mr. MCCORMACK. Let me ask this one question while you're still here. Dr. Swisher, really we are essentially into engineering, are we not, engineering applications of hydrogen?

Dr. SWISHER. Yes, we are, on certain aspects of hydrogen technology.

Mr. MCCORMACK. Any time we get into engineering, then we can control the rate of program development. It isn't a matter of waiting for the right answer from a research program.

Dr. Swisher. That's correct.

Mr. McCormack. If we put the money in, we can get the programs moving because we are actually into engineering itself, and not just basic research. We may be in basic research on hydrogen production for, let's say thermochemical systems, but it seems to me there's an important distinction here. Really, I want to come to your rescue in a sense, as far as your programs are concerned.

It seems to me that, in this phase at least, the use of hydrogen, since it is fundamentally an engineering program, that we could speed it up and get good results sooner by funding it at higher levels. Is that a fair statement?

Dr. Swisher. Yes, it is a fair statement.

Mr. Ottinger. What are the prime uses that you see in the near term?

Dr. Swisher. We are looking at the possible tie of hydrogen production to low hydro sources, particularly in New England for use as a chemical feedstock. We are trying to keep the pace we had set a year or so ago on that program. We are going to take another look at the production of hydrogen using offpeak electrical power for injection into the natural gas pipeline system. We think that is a possible near-term item.

In general we try to tie our technology base around some of these applications with near-term potential, even though the market impact is modest, to help us prepare for the big splash by the year 2000 when it will be more competitive with alternate fuels.

Mr. McCormack. Thank you, Mr. Chairman.

Mr. Ottinger. I want to thank you all very much.

Mr. McCormack. I have a couple more questions here. I would like to ask any one of the panelists to comment in response to Dr. Swisher's most recent statement about load leveling. I would like to ask how you would compare the projected time line for load leveling using hydrogen as compared to using superconducting storage of electricity.

Dr. Kane?

Dr. Kane. I'll just risk an answer. I guess I wouldn't put too much authority, but I think superconducting systems are much further away than hydrogen. I could probably sit down and put together the elements of an offpeak storage system using hydrogen, and I believe every one of them would be at an engineering level.

Mr. McCormack. So you think that is at an engineering level whereas the cryogenic storage is still at the demonstration level perhaps?

Dr. Kane. With difficulty. As you certainly know, Mr. Congressman, cryogenic systems are doable and are being done today in special situations, but they are certainly not an item of commerce on the scale it would take to store large amounts of energy.

Now, again, perhaps I stuck in my oar, and there would be other members of the panel who would care to comment.

Dr. Gregory. I believe if you wanted to build a liquid hydrogen offpeak storage system you could do it. You could go out and order the equipment and build it now. I think there is a scale up to level and size of equipment that may not have been built before, but I think it could be done. It would be expensive and it would have a round-trip efficiency of something like 25 percent. You only get about a quarter of the energy back that you put in by the time you've gone through the whole cycle. We need research to improve that efficiency and lower the price, but you could do it. I think I would say that we could probably do it in an economical, viable, and attractive way within 5 to 10 years. I don't see that with superconducting systems.

Mr. McCormack. You wouldn't say that load leveling with hydrogen would be economically competitive only if you didn't have anything else at all available?

Dr. Gregory. It has to depend on what the price of the off-peak power is and what you can get for it when you sell it back again. I think the difference between those two costs is increasing all the time. At the present time it would not be economic, but even the same technology is going to be more economical 25 years from now because of that difference in price. We could run through a demonstration of underground storage of hydrogen in aquifer system using the technology that you use now for natural gas, and I think that would be a successful demonstration of what we know now. And by that method you could store hydrogen much more efficiently. But the first one of those storage systems is going to require a very heavy capital investment in hydrogen gas. The biggest single cost item there is the gas you put into the system.

Mr. McCormack. Do you feel that the knowledge you would gain from a successful demonstration of hydrogen storage underground could be extrapolated to a different site or would we encounter the same problems we encountered with geothermal energy where a facility that works one place may not work a mile away because the geology is different.

Dr. Gregory. I think the experience of the natural gas industry in storing gas in different geographic locations is enough to be able to extrapolate hydrogen from one place to another. I think the analogy with gas storage is good enough.

Mr. McCormack. So the fact that the hydrogen is a much smaller molecule and more difficult to contain doesn't seem to disturb you.

Dr. Gregory. It doesn't seem to be more difficult to contain hydrogen in an underground structure than natural gas. The things that seal the gas in don't really care what kind of gas it is.

Mr. McCormack. Thank you.

One of you gentlemen I think mentioned something about using metal hydrides for the storage of hydrogen and I missed that. I would like to pick up one thing.

Dr. Mezzina. That was probably me, and what I said was that the bulk hydride storage, bulk hydride hydrogen storage, proves, at least based on current materials and current materials costs, to be totally uneconomical.

Mr. McCormack. I see, it does work?

Dr. Mezzina. It does work.

Mr. McCormack. When you say uneconomical——

Dr. Mezzina. Iron-titanium hydride as compared to, say, compressed gas or compared to liquefied.

Mr. McCormack. Economically it is not practical at the present time?

Dr. Mezzina. Right. We are talking about factors of 2 to 4 differences.

Mr. McCormack. We are also talking about heavy weights.

Dr. Mezzina. When you raise the question as to specificity regarding an application, metal hydrides will offer you the equivalent volume—you can store hydrogen in the equivalent volume that you can—for example, liquid hydrogen—but with a weight penalty. As far as weight, it—metal hydride—will be around 10 to 20 percent better than you would find in any compressed gas system.

Mr. McCormack. Let me put the question another way. I can see the possibility, if we could make it economically competitive and effective, to use a metal hydride system for automobiles, for surface transportation.

Dr. Mezzina. Certainly.

Mr. McCormack. But you might run into problems using it with the airplane?

Dr. Mezzina. You would want to address the problem of improving cost and higher storage capacity probably by a factor of 2 over what we are having today.

Mr. McCormack. What about weight for airplanes, does this present a problem?

Dr. Mezzina. Hydrides for airplanes, no.

Mr. McCormack. Hydrides are out of the question for airplanes.

Dr. Mezzina. Out of the question.

Mr. McCormack. That's what I want to get at.

Dr. Swisher, I got the impression you were comparing flywheels, batteries, and thermal storage to hydrogen as a propulsion system; is that correct?

Dr. Swisher. They compete budgetwise.

Mr. McCormack. But they don't compete in distance——

Dr. Swisher. In distance?

Mr. McCormack. In the amount of energy you can store in a vehicle, let's say an automobile.

Let me express my position here so you will understand my question. As you know, I am the sponsor of our electric vehicle program, and I'm pushing as hard as I can on battery research. I think all of these things are great, and I want to push them as fast as I can, but I conceive of them all having that one limitation, range; that is, the total amount of energy you can put in. That limitation presumably wouldn't apply in the case of hydrogen as a hydride or as a liquid fuel. You could get a good deal more range out of a tank of hydrogen as a hydride or a liquid than you could expect to get, at least in the foreseeable future, out of any of the existing electric vehicle systems. Am I miscalculating?

Dr. Swisher. You can get more distance out of a hydrogen vehicle than you can out of a battery-powered vehicle. With today's batteries there's no question.

Mr. McCormack. Do you think that battery research brings us into the range of competitiveness with hydrogen?

Dr. Swisher. The advanced batteries do make them competitive.

Mr. McCormack. That includes thermal batteries, the storage of heat as heat?

Dr. Swisher. We are not working on thermal storage for transportation systems.

Mr. McCormack. Are you aware of the thermal batteries that have been investigated by Harford? Heat storage in graphite?

Dr. Swisher. That idea came to us sometime ago. We did have some contracts on what we call thermal batteries tied to Sterling engines a few years ago, but it just didn't seem as if our priority should be to continue to support that area.

Mr. McCormack. Is this in your area of responsibility?

Dr. Swisher. I have responsibility for thermal storage.

Mr. McCormack. Would you mind preparing a one-page commentary, a casual, informal commentary, comparing what you project as the practicality of thermal storage in graphite for automobile propulsion as compared to the best battery storage systems we now have?

Dr. Swisher. I'd be glad to do that.

[The material referred to follows:]

INFORMATION ON HEAT STORAGE

"BATTERIES" FOR STIRLING ENGINE

PAST DOE EFFORT

In 1976 a project was initiated to evaluate thermal energy storage with a
heat engine for highway vehicle propulsion. The project was co-funded by
DOE's Transportation Energy Conservation Division and Energy Storage Systems
Division, and implemented by Argonne National Laboratory (ANL). Two concep-
tual designs were prepared by ANL subcontractors. Both used phase change
storage and a Stirling engine. The concept prepared by Sigma Research
employed LiF/MgF$_2$ eutectic; Thermo Electron studied both a LiF (single
medium) and an NaF/MgF$_2$ eutectic.

ANL also participated in the DOE funded technical analysis of energy storage
systems for automobile propulsion conducted by Lawrence Livermore Laboratory.
That study evaluated electric batteries, thermal storage, hydrogen storage
and flywheels. The reports indicated that thermal storage for vehicle propulsion is feasible (General Motors actually built such a car in 1964, the
"Calvair", a modified Corvair with a Stirling engine and sensible heat
storage in alumina). While the data indicate potential for weight, initial
cost, and life cycle cost reductions in comparison to lead/acid batteries,
thermal storage (with optimistic data) was only marginally competitive with
other advanced storage devices for vehicles (with realistic data). Funding
for continued development was not available and the project was terminated
in 1979.

A RECENT PROPOSAL

Hanford Engineering Development Laboratory (HEDL) claims that thermal storage
with Stirling engines is better than advanced batteries. Their approach
employs sensible heat storage in graphite (or other media) with temperatures
up to 2000°C (3632°F). This office has been in contact with HEDL, received
their data and discussed their concept (which they claim is proprietary).
A quick review of the previous work and the HEDL concept was conducted.

The HEDL approach does offer the potential for significant improvements over
the previous thermal storage work by Sigma Research and Thermo Electron.
However, compared to advanced battery energy storage concepts, the HEDL
thermal storage concept would at best offer only modest weight and volume
advantages. Cost data for the HEDL concept are too uncertain to assess at
this time. Safety is a problem for the HEDL concept because of the potential

for combustion of the storage media and for fires started from contact with the very high temperature storage media.

In summary, the HEDL concept has potential for improvement over previous thermal storage developments, but is not likely to be better than other advanced devices for vehicles. As such, this thermal storage concept might be considered as a back-up to other approaches. Although the developers claim the concept can be developed very rapidly, there are substantial risks and uncertainties yet to be resolved.

Mr. McCORMACK. Don't feel constrained to make it a professional paper. I just want to get myself in the ballpark on that subject.

Dr. SWISHER. OK.

Mr. McCORMACK. Dr. Kane, I notice in your expenditure on hydrogen dissociation you show no end-use funds for fuel cells; in other words, you don't show any funds for technologies for burning, for instance, ammonia as a fuel. Can you comment on that?

Dr. KANE. Yes, Congressman, while you were out I commented that there's a major effort on fuel cells in the fossil-energy program and much of that is applicable because most of them use a reformer to take the hydrocarbons to hydrogen and carbon monoxide, so most of the current fuel cells are actually hydrogen burners. So I think a lot of their research, which I didn't tabulate here, is applicable to the same kinds of questions we'll face.

In addition to that, I believe Dr. Swisher has a small amount of work on fuel cells which I inadvertently put in his electrolysis number at the top of the budget. I have it shown as 3.3. Jim, can you clarify this point?

Dr. SWISHER. I'm not even sure that it comes in our part of the program. We have a few hundred thousand dollars in fuel cells only.

Mr. McCORMACK. United Technology, for instance, is trying to build fuel cells. What are they using for fuel?

Dr. KANE. Methane.

Mr. McCORMACK. Is anyone working on using ammonia? If we are going to have OTEC systems making ammonia, wouldn't a logical end-use for that ammonia be for fuel cells?

Dr. KANE. I think maybe I'll pass that one on to Dr. Gregory. Of course, the United Technology one goes back to support by the gas people, and methane was the goal at that time. Natural gas was the goal, more correctly.

I think there is no technical reason why an ammonia fuel cell couldn't be made, but I certainly am going to defer to people who know more about it on both sides perhaps.

Dr. GREGORY. I understand that the fossil-energy fuel cell programs are looking at methane, naphtha, and coal as fuel supplies for their cells. Of course, you have to convert them to a hydrogen-rich gas before the fuel cell will accept it. The fuel cell really burns hydrogen but an integrated plant is a black box that has fossil fuel going in and electricity coming out.

Mr. McCORMACK. Including the reformer?

Dr. GREGORY. Including the reformer. I don't know of any experimental work that is going on at the present time in using ammonia as a fuel cell fuel. Some of the paper studies that were done by IGT and others, in looking at the potential for ocean thermal energy, included a look at the various ways of transporting energy from a floating platform to an enduse. And one of the concepts that was compared to the others was ammonia being brought ashore in tankers and fed into a fuel cell.

Mr. McCORMACK. I would assume in this instance the fuel cell would take the ammonia directly, wouldn't it?

Dr. GREGORY. It would require cracking to hydrogen and nitrogen.

Mr. McCORMACK. A fuel cell simply won't take the pure ammonia.

Dr. GREGORY. No.

Mr. McCORMACK. I regret that that bit of information comes out that way.

Finally, Dr Kane, you talked about the notion that there is no great urgency in certain aspects of the hydrogen program. I have two questions. First of all, I take it that given the existing technology for photovoltaics you could prepare a fairly good estimate of the cost of making hydrogen from a remotized, desert photovoltaic system, just simply an automated station that would sit there and when it had enough sunlight would turn itself on and make hydrogen and when the Sun goes down, turn itself off and wait until the next day, then make some more. Have you ever tried to determine what the cost of hydrogen would be using today's state-of-the-art photovoltaic systems?

Dr. KANE. I have not; no.

Mr. McCORMACK. Would it be possible to make a back-of-the-envelope calculation to try to get us in the ballpark?

Dr. KANE. It certainly seems reasonable to me because every component photovoltaic puts out d.c. which is what you need for electrolysis and it puts it out in a voltage range that's kind of convenient, and I think the prices could be—Dr. Swisher looks nervous. Maybe he has done that kind of thing.

Mr. McCORMACK. Have you?

Dr. SWISHER. I haven't done the calculation, but an organization came to us recently that had done some calculations. What they said was, if we reached the goals in development of photovoltaic devices at 50 cents or $1 per watt, we should be able to make hydrogen for $6 to $8 per 1 million Btu, which makes some sense.

Mr. McCORMACK. May I say, Dr. Swisher, that I don't expect us to reach those goals in the foreseeable future. I don't think we will reach them in this decade, and I'm not sure we will reach them in this century. I think they are overly optimistic. I would prefer that you work with something that would be closer to realism and do a series of calculations at $4 a watt, $2 a watt, and $1 a watt. I wouldn't go below $1 a watt for photovoltaics, because I don't think we're going to get there.

Dr. SWISHER. I don't know the answer to that set of calculations, but I do know that if the numbers are higher, then it will be somewhat futuristic as far as commercialization potential.

Mr. McCORMACK. I have one final question for you, Dr. Kane, and I would be happy to have anyone else comment on this, and that is: Serious consideration of a more aggressive program for hydrogen production from thermochemical decomposition of water. We have our high-temperature, gas-cooled nuclear plants coming along now. That program has been funded at $40 million for this year and one of the areas of major application is going to be process heat. We also have the temperatures that we have today from conventional nuclear power-plants and from other industrial processes where you may have smaller amounts of higher temperature heat that could be made available. I think there is a degree of urgency for us to have at least a good fix on what we could do in terms of producing large quantities of hydrogen in the relatively near future using existing technologies and perferably waste heat and water as a source of energy input.

In other words, what could we do and how soon could we do it? What would the cost be? What is the best system? I understand we have computer runs on dozens of different thermochemical processes. What would the best system be and what would be a systems analysis on the entire program? Maybe it is too big a project and maybe it is not well enough defined. Maybe it needs to be refined before we ask for it, but I think it is something that Members of the Congress are going to be asking for in the very near future. I would like to ask you to comment on it if you can now and maybe you would like to think about it.

Dr. KANE. I will make a comment. I think there are other people here perhaps at least two that I know of who would be willing to make a comment.

To get a fix on a technology that we currently don't have a good fix on. Dr. Funk went through this in quite some detail. We don't have a good fix on the actual scaled up cost of thermal water splitting, so there is some urgency to get that fixed, I would agree with that.

An urgency to produce hydrogen by known technology to show we can do it is what I don't usually agree with. As you pointed out earlier, the efficiency of these cycles becomes really good when you go to a very high temperature source, such as the gas-cooled reactor. They look less and less interesting, I believe, as you go to waste heat, because although the waste heat may cost you very little, the thermal efficiency of the cycle has dropped so low that the capital costs will eventually get to you. That's the problem.

I have a feeling that we're not going to learn much more about thermochemical water splitting by dreaming up more cycles. I think what's going to be needed is some kind of a demonstration that will try to get costs on a real operating system. I don't know what scale it has to be. I'm not an engineer. But today I'm kind of overwhelmed with a sense of I don't really have any idea whether thermal water splitting is just kind of a scientific curiosity or a real lead toward a way we could produce hydrogen. I think there are at least two other people at the table who are anxious to give an opinion on that.

Derek, you are one of those I am speaking of.

Dr. GREGORY. Some years ago we ran a comparison of the efficiency of hydrogen production from heat, using the thermochemical route and using the electrolysis route. We assumed that all our wildest dreams came true—we took the best cycles we had developed on paper and briefly checked out in the lab and we took electrolysis figures from some of the more optimistic projections of General Electric and Teledyne.

Our overall conclusion was if you have heat at temperatures less than about 600° Celsius on an efficiency basis, it is better to go through the electrolysis than the thermochemical route. Now in the years since we did that we haven't seen anything that has radically changed that position. And since we don't have technology today that generates nuclear heat at above 600° Celsius—I think you asked your question relating to today's technology—we would go through the electrolysis route to generate power in a conventional way and run an electrolyzer.

If you talk about waste heat from the nuclear reactor, the engineers who are trying to generate electric power wring so much energy out of that heat that by the time it gets to the "waste" stage it is useless for almost anything. There is a lot of it. but you really wouldn't be able to use it for making hydrogen.

Let me come back to this 600°C point. That might be up or down by 100°, but we don't have reactors today in operation, commercially proven, that can generate heat at a high enough temperature in my opinion to justify a thermochemical process. The work we have been doing on thermochemical processes at IGT and the work other people have been doing tends to look at the 800° Celsius area which is the upper limit that the nuclear engineers tell us they will be able to get to with the HTGR. At that point we can, on an efficiency basis, beat electrolysis. We don't know what the costs are.

Mr. McCORMACK. Could the process be synthesized using a pilot plant with natural gas as a source of heat?

Dr. GREGORY. Yes it could. There's no reason why you couldn't build a process development unit using a synthetic heat source, a gas heater, and you would learn a lot about the thermochemical cycle you are trying to develop.

Mr. McCORMACK. It would take a number of years, wouldn't it, just to do that?

Dr. GREGORY. Yes.

Mr. McCORMACK. Putting it in parallel with HTGR development might not be a total waste of time.

Dr. GREGORY. That's correct, and I think that is the position that we and many others have been taking. I think you heard today (from Dr. Funk) that the technology of thermochemical hydrogen is not limited by the chemical technology but by the technology of the heat source itself and so it would make sense in the long term to develop both the heat source and the chemistry.

Mr. McCORMACK. Dr. Swisher?

Dr. SWISHER. I agree with the comments that were made by the others. I would like to add one thing and that is the world leaders in the thermochemical hydrogen production area are in Europe. We work with them through an international agreement. They are proceeding with an engineering process development unit, which they hope to complete in about 3 years. We will be able to benefit from the results of their tests. But it is very difficult to get a good handle on it at the present time.

Mr. McCORMACK. Which countries are primarily involved?

Dr. SWISHER. It is the ISPRA Laboratory of the Commission of the European Communities, so it is the laboratory that is funded by many European countries.

Mr. McCORMACK. As you know, by the way, our high temperature gas-cooled reactor program is undertaken jointly with Germany and they are looking at the HTGR as a source of process heat and so are the Japanese.

I think I have exhausted my questions. Do any of you have any comments you would like to put on the record?

(No response.)

If any of you have any additional information you would like to submit, we would appreciate it. If you are prepared to do so, we have some questions we would like to submit in writing that you might answer at your leisure, if that's OK with you.

I want to thank you all very much. As I said when we started, I think this hearing is the beginning of a fairly important legislative process that will lead us to deeper involvement with not only the production of hydrogen and the development of technologies for its storage and use but the use of hydrogen to relieve our present dependence upon imported oil and on fossil fuels. This will not only lead to greater energy independence for this country but to a cleaner environment, both of which are highly desirable goals. I thank you all very much.

[Whereupon, at 5:10 p.m., the joint subcommittee hearing was concluded.]

APPENDIX

Dr. James Kane, Associate Director
Office of Energy Research
U.S. Department of Energy
Washington, D.C. 20585

Dear Dr. Kane:

I appreciate the testimony you presented to the Subcommittee on June 25. Enclosed are additional questions for the record.

Question 1: In 1979, the annual consumption of industrial hydrogen was approximately 3 trillion standard cubic feet. It is expected to triple by the year 2000. Most of this industrial hydrogen was made from natural gas and accounted for 3% of the total U.S. hydrogen consumption in 1979. The majority of individual hydrogen consumers required less than 100 million standard cubic feet per day. Since this is smaller than that generally considered practical for syngas plants, many will elect to install electrolytic plants. Therefore, couldn't much of the natural gas burden be shifted to coal or electric power in the next few years through the direct electrolysis of water, beginning immediately with the highly dispersed small user segment? Also, what considerations are being given to shifting the industrial process hydrogen load to alternative fuels?

Question 2: Current International Energy Agency agreements dictate that the U.S. play a lead role in the development of the Solid Polymer Electrolyte technology, whereas the Europeans and Canadians are expected to develop the alkaline electrolysis technology. In point of fact however, the U.S. leads the Europeans in the development of practical and efficient alkaline electrolyzers. Are we not in danger of losing this advantage under the present agreements, with the consequence that U.S. manufacturers will be at a disadvantage with respect to foreign equipment? Shouldn't the two comparable technologies receive equitable U.S. support?

Question 3: What role could ammonia derived from hydrogen play in transportation and storage systems? What advantage would it have over metal hydrides or cyrogenic storage? What efforts are being made by DOE to fund fuel cells which use ammonia as a feedstock?

Sincerely,

RICHARD L. OTTINGER
Chairman

CC: Hon. Clarence D. Long
    Jim Martin, DOE

Department of Energy .
Washington, D.C. **20585**

July 21, 1980

Dear Ms. Davis:

Attached you will find the answers to questions submitted
for the record by James Kane, Associate Director for the
Office of Basic Energy Science, Department of Energy, for
the hearing before the Committee on Science and Technology,
Subcommittee on Energy Development and Application on
June 25, 1980.

If you have any questions please do not hesitate to contact me
directly on 252-5777.

Sincerely,

Frank R. Pagnotta
Director
Office of The Secretary

Ms. Regina Davis
Committee on Science and
   Technology
Subcommittee on Energy
   Development and Application
Room 2321, RHOB
Washington, D.C.   20515

Answers to Questions from the Hearing on
"Hydrogen: Production and End Uses" on June 25, 1980

Subcommittee on Energy Development and Application
House Committee of Science and Technology

Question 1:

In 1979, the annual consumption of industrial hydrogen was approximately 3 trillion
standard cubic feet. It is expected to triple by the year 2000. Most of this
industrial hydrogen was made from natural gas and accounted for 3% of the total
U.S. natural gas consurption in 1979. The majority of individual hydrogen consumer
required less than 100 million standard cubic feet per day. Since this is smaller
than that generally considered practical for syngas plants, many will elect to
install electrolytic plants. Therefore, couldn't much of the natural gas burden
be shifted to coal or electric power in the next few years through the direct
electrolysis of water, beginning immediately with the highly dispersed small
user segment? Also, what considerations are being given to shifting the industrial
process hydrogen load to alternative fuels?

Answer:

In this question the point is raised with respect to the advisability of shifting

the jurisdiction of industrial hydrogen from natural gas to the electrolysis of

water. My comments on the matter are as follows:

Unless this shift is mandated by the government, the user of hydrogen will base

his decision on economics plus some added factor based on reliability of the supply

Most current users prefer to purchase gaseous or liquid hydrogen, rather than

electrolyze. There are certainly exceptions, where cheap electric power or high

transportation costs for hydrogen influence the decision. Increased natural gas

costs and/or its reduced availability could provide incentives to small user

hydrogen markets for installing on-site water electrolysis systems provided the

electric generating capacity is available at competitive costs. Reduced

electrolyzer capital cost and higher electrolyzer operating efficiencies coupled

to system designs which minimize operating complexity while attaining high

performance reliability must be demonstrated before these markets can materialize

significantly. These issues and problems are now being addressed in the

electrolytic hydrogen production programs supported by DOE.

Since the natural gas act of 1978, increased drilling has led to significant additions to our gas reserves, although the price has also risen. It appears then that our supply of natural gas is not nearly as precarious as that of petroleum. Since the price of electricity has risen at least as rapidly as that of gas, the economics appear to favor the continued production of hydrogen from methane.

If the shift to electrolysis were mandated, it could result in problems due to shortages in the supply of electricity. Reserve margins for electricity are quite moderate throughout the U.S. today, and shortages are predicted by some. Additional capacity will be slowed by the hiatus in nuclear generation, and by the necessity that the utilities use their resources to convert gas and petroleum burning plants to coal. Surplus electricity for electrolysis may just not be available.

I, therefore, conclude that the shift of hydrogen from methane to electrolysis is not apt to happen in the next decade, and should not be required.

In the longer run, this may not be true. The cost of methane may well continue to rise, while the cost of electricity from coal or nuclear sources may stabilize At this time, conversion to electrolysis will take place.

137

Question 2:

Current International Energy Agency agreements dictate that the U.S. play a lead
role in the development of the Solid Polymer Electrolyte technology, whereas the
Europeans and Canadians are expected to develop the alkaline electrolysis
technology. In point of fact however, the U.S. leads the Europeans in the
development of practical and efficient alkaline electrolyzers. Are we not
in danger of losing this advantage under the present agreements, with the
consequence that U.S. manufacturers will be at a disadvantage with respect
to foreign equipment? Shouldn't the two comparable technologies receive
equitable U.S. support?

Answer:

The premise that the U.S. leads the Europeans in the development of practical

and efficient alkaline electrolyzers is, at a minimum, arguable. European-based

electrolyzer manufacturers such as Norsk-Hydro, Brown-Boveri Corporation, and

Lurgi, have been leaders in the alkaline electrolyzer industry for some time,

especially for large multi-megawatt systems. This position was attained due

to availability of substantial hydroelectric resources (e.g., Norway) coupled

with the lack of indigenous natural gas resources to meet demands for hydrogen

as a chemical and agricultural commodity. The U.S. alkaline electrolyzer

industry has addressed smaller user and specialty markets.

The Solid Polymer Electrolyte (SPE) technology is new and has never been used

on a large scale. It is projected to offer significant improvements in both

energy efficiency and lower capital costs over alkaline units. The risk,

however, is greater and, therefore, government funding has focused on the

SPE developments.

Recent efforts on alkaline systems under DOE sponsorship have identified potential

advances in catalyst, electrode and materials development which may also upgrade

system efficiencies and reduce capital costs. The present R&D effort needed on

alkaline electrolysis is a relatively straightforward effort to improve

commercially available technology. Therefore the lead role for the alkaline

systems in the U.S. is in the industrial sector rather than the Government.

The current International Energy Agency agreement is intended to be a means

for providing maximum leverage to U.S. R&D expenditures.

Question 3:

(a) What role could ammonia derived from hydrogen play in transportation and storage systems? (b) What advantage would it have over metal hydrides or cyrogenic storage? (c) What efforts are being made by DOE to fund fuel cells which use ammonia as a feedstock?

Answer:

(a) Ammonia has been considered as a fuel candidate for internal combustion engines for many years. It can be burned in engines directly or reformed to produce hydrogen gas as fuel.

Ammonia has the advantage of being a liquid fuel which leads directly to water and nitrogen as the primary products of combustion. The principal disadvantages of the direct use of ammonia in engines include the low specific net heating value (8000 Btu/lb as compared to 19,300 for gasoline), emission of oxides of nitrogen, energy consumption to synthesize the ammonia and increased complexity of engine systems. Though the handling, transporting and storage of ammonia is established practice commercially, it does have the potential for safety and environmental problems as a widespread consumer product. Ammonia can be cracked to hydrogen and nitrogen prior to combustion. This case has the same advantages and disadvantages as for the direct combustion except for the oxides of nitrogen emissions. In this case, one must also be concerned with energy consumption in the reforming step. Although, exhaust heat can be used as a heat source, supplemental energy will be needed during cold-start and warmup and during cold weather operation. The need for supplemental energy for some operations further increases system complexities.

Other fuel candidates, such as hydrocarbons and alcohols from shale, coal, biomass and waste materials appear at the present time to be more attractive alternatives than ammonia.

(b) Ammonia is, of course, more easily stored than a cryogenic liquid such as hydrogen because of its physical properties, especially lower volatility. It is also lighter in weight to comparable metal hydride storage systems. Accordingly, it is also less expensive to store and transport than the currently available alternatives for hydrogen.

(c) Fuel cells are normally fueled by hydrogen and oxygen. The oxygen usually is supplied from air. The hydrogen can be supplied by any form of hydrogen storage (compressed gas, cryogenic liquid, hydrides) or by thermally "cracking" ammonia or any hydrocarbon (such as methane from natural gas or naptha from petroleum). The technology for thermal cracking of ammonia already exists. Thus no special DOE effort is needed other than existing efforts to develop improved fuel cells and continuing analytic studies of environmental, safety, and energy balance comparisons between ammonia and other ways of supplying hydrogen to fuel cells.

In certain applications, such as Ocean Thermal Energy Conversion (OTEC), the ammonia production and transport option must be given serious consideration. This is especially true when cruise ships or platforms are located substantial distances from shore making energy transmission by wire impractical.

There have been efforts in the past (Allis Chalmers) where ammonia, as a direct feed to fuel cells, was investigated. Results did not appear promising except for systems which would employ a "pre-cracking step". Energy efficiency and cost considerations, compared to steam reforming of other hydrocarbons (natural or synthetic), will dictate the applicability of the concept.

          .˅cS

B-374 RA┐.- ._-c OFFICE BUILDING

WASHINGTON, D.C. 20515

July 1, 1980

Dr. James Kane, Associate Director
Office of Energy Research
U.S. Department of Energy
Washington, D.C. 20585

Dear Dr. Kane:

I appreciate the testimony you presented to the Subcommittee on June 25.
Enclosed are additional questions for the record.

Question 1: In 1979, the annual consumption of industrial hydrogen was
approximately 3 trillion standard cubic feet. It is expected to triple
by the year 2000. Most of this industrial hydrogen was made from natural
gas and accounted for 3% of the total U.S. hydrogen consumption in 1979.
The majority of individual hydrogen consumers required less than 100 million standard cubic feet per day. Since this is smaller than that generally considered practical for syngas plants, many will elect to install electrolytic plants. Therefore, couldn't much of the natural gas burden be
shifted to coal or electric power in the next few years through the direct
electrolysis of water, beginning immediately with the highly dispersed small
user segment? Also, what considerations are being given to shifting the
industrial process hydrogen load to alternative fuels?

Question 2: Current International Energy Agency agreements dictate that the
U.S. play a lead role in the development of the Solid Polymer Electrolyte
technology, whereas the Europeans and Canadians are expected to develop the
alkaline electrolysis technology. In point of fact however, the U.S. leads
the Europeans in the development of practical and efficient alkaline electrolyzers. Are we not in danger of losing this advantage under the present
agreements, with the consequence that U.S. manufacturers will be at a disadvantage with respect to foreign equipment? Shouldn't the two comparable
technologies receive equitable U.S. support?

Question 3: What role could ammonia derived from hydrogen play in transportation and storage systems? What advantage would it have over metal
hydrides or cyrogenic storage? What efforts are being made by DOE to fund
fuel cells which use ammonia as a feedstock?

Sincerely,

RICHARD L. OTTINGER
Chairman

CC: Hon. Clarence D. Long
     Jim Martin, DOE

CLARENCE D. LONG
2D DISTRICT, MARYLAND

COMMITTEE ON
APPROPRIATIONS

CHAIRMAN:
SUBCOMMITTEE ON
FOREIGN OPERATIONS

MEMBER:
SUBCOMMITTEES ON
INTERIOR

MILITARY CONSTRUCTION

Congress of the United States
House of Representatives
Washington, D.C. 20515

2407 RAYBURN BUILDING
WASHINGTON, D C 20515
(202) 225-3061

DISTRICT OFFICE:
200 POST OFFICE BUILDING
CHESAPEAKE AND
WASHINGTON AVENUES
TOWSON, MARYLAND 21204
(301) 828-6616

"OFFICE ON WHEELS"

June 24, 1980

The Honorable Richard L. Ottinger
Chairman
Subcommittee on Energy Development and Applications
B374 Rayburn House Office Building
Washington, D.C. 20515

Dear Dick

I would appreciate it if you would permit the following questions to be submitted for the record during your June 25, 1980 hearing on hydrogen

Question 1.   In 1979, the annual consumption of industrial hydrogen was approximately 3 trillion standard cubic feet. It is expected to triple by the year 2000. Most of this industrial hydrogen was made from natural gas and accounted for 3% of the total U.S. hydrogen consumption in 1979. The majority of individual hydrogen consumers required less than 100 million standard cubic feet per day. Since this is smaller than that generally considered practical for syngas plants, many will elect to install electrolytic plants. Therefore, couldn't much of the natural gas burden be shifted to coal or electric power in the next few years through the direct electrolysis of water, beginning immediately with the highly dispersed small user segment? Also, what considerations are being given to shifting the industrial process hydrogen load to alternative fuels?

Question 2.   Current International Energy Agency agreements dictate that the U.S. play a lead role in the development of the Solid Polymer Electrolyte technology, whereas the Europeans and Canadians are expected to develop the alkaline electrolysis technology. In point of fact however, the U.S. leads the Europeans in the development of practical and efficient alkaline electrolyzers. Are we not in danger of losing this advantage under the present agreements, with the consequence that U.S. manufacturers will be at a disadvantage with respect to foreign equipment? Shouldn't the two comparable technologies receive equitable U.S. support?

Warm regards,

CLARENCE D. LONG

CDL cas

142

UNIVERSITY OF KENTUCKY

LEXINGTON KENTUCKY 40506

SOCIATE VICE PRESIDENT
OR ACADEMIC AFFAIRS
NATOR OF ENERGY RESEARCH

206 ADMINISTRATION BUILDING
PHONE (606) 258 8636

August 7, 1980

Dr. David Eck
Subcommittee on Energy
 Development and Applications
Committee on Science and Technology
U.S. House of Representatives
B-374 Rayburn House Office Building
Washington, D.C. 20515

Dear Dr. Eck:

At the June 25th hearing on "Hydrogen: Production and
Energy Uses" a question came up concerning work performed by
the Billings Energy Corporation. I mentioned that I was chairman of the review group and perhaps it was not clear that I
meant the group which reviewed the seminar held at Snowbird,
Utah on June 11-15, 1979. I have attached for your information
a copy of the review group report along with a copy of a letter
from one of the members to me. I would like to make it clear
that this group did not review the preliminary draft of the report prepared by Billings. Our comments apply to what we observed
during the seminar and the comments I made at the hearing re-
flected my impression of that seminar and did not apply to any
report prepared by Billings. I hope you will make this clear to
the members of the subcommittee, especially Congressman Gore.

Very truly yours,

James E. Funk
Associate Vice President

JEF/n

Attachments

UNIVERSITY OF KENTUCKY

LEXINGTON, KENTUCKY 40506

SOCIATE VICE PRESIDENT
OR ACADEMIC AFFAIRS
INATOR OF ENERGY RESEARCH

206 ADM NISTRATION E
PHONE (606) 258 |

MEMORANDUM

August 29, 1979

TO: K. Ekman
        A. Kashani
        J. O'Hara

FROM: James E. Funk

You will find attached a copy of what I hope is the
final version of our report on the Hydrogen from Coal Cost
Estimation Seminar. I have made some editorial changes and
have appended Karl Ekman's letter. If any of you have any
problems with any of this please let me and/or Joe Hanson
know as soon as possible. If I don't hear from anyone within
two weeks I'll assume that we have completed our job and that
Joe Hanson has the final report in his hands.

cc: C. England
     J. Hanson
     J. Kelley
     G. Varsi

JEF/n

Attachment

REVIEW GROUP REPORT

Hydrogen from Coal Cost Estimation Seminar
Snowbird, Utah
June 11-15, 1979
Conducted by the Billings Energy Corporation

Members of the Review Group: Karl R. Ekman, JPL; James E. Funk,
University of Kentucky; Ali Kashani, JPL: and James O'Hara,
Ralph M. Parsons Company.

The task of the Review Group was to review and comment on
the materials presented at this Cost Estimation Seminar, especially in view of two questions posed by Roger Billings at the
beginning of the seminar.

1.   Is it technically feasible to produce hydrogen
from coal?

2.   If so, what is the range of costs involved?

The Review Group answered the first question in the affirma-
tive. There is no doubt that it is technically feasible to produce
hydrogen from coal; coal gasification has been accomplished often
in the past although not yet in the U.S. with modern technology on
a large scale basis.

The Review Group wishes to offer the following general remarks.

1.   We strongly support the objective of the Cost Estimation Seminar, although we would like to re-emphasize
the scope and complexity of the task. The production
plants in question are very large and very complicated
and it is quite easy to underestimate the total capital
and operating costs involved due to the lack of experience with the operation of such facilities. This
point is made in more detail in the attached letter
from one of the members of the Review Group.

145

2. The concept of clearly showing the various components of the capital cost employed in the Billings computer model is well accepted, and should serve the purpose here quite well.

3. It is the objective of the national energy plan to move coal into energy-consuming sectors now served by oil and natural gas. In 1976 to 1978, however, the share of the U.S. energy market served by coal dropped from 19.2% to 18.1%. Hydrogen from coal is a means by which coal can be used in a broader way, and it is more attractive environmentally than direct combustion.

The Review Group offers the following specific comments. We would like to emphasize that the numbers and results calculated and presented at this seminar should be used for planning and intercomparison purposes. A great deal more work as well as site-specific data are required before the numbers can be considered for use in an absolute sense.

1. The final production costs for 100 x 10^6 SCF/day H_2 presented by Exxon and K-T are in quite good agreement.

2. We agree qualitatively with the trend of cost with plant size as presented by K-T.

3. For large plants, numbers have been presented for two commercially demonstrated technologies. It will be highly desirable to obtain equivalent estimates for other technologies and from other contractors.

4. We wish to reiterate the importance of the plant operating factor on the final production cost, a point which was strongly made by more than one of the speakers.

5. In the context of implementing the analysis described in the specialty analysis blue book presented by Billings, there are a number of key project parameters which have yet to be accurately and quantitatively defined. Examples are coal cost, transportation cost, financing cost, and a realistic projection of inflation rate.

6. We wish to emphasize and reiterate that it is very
   important to be sure that all costs associated with
   environmental considerations are taken into account.
   For example, solid waste disposal, atmospheric and
   water contaminants.

7. The plant capital investment estimates presented by
   K-T and Exxon seem to be credible and we feel that
   they are certainly suitable for use in planning and
   intercomparison.

8. Four cases run on the computer were made available
   to us, and the costs ranged from $3.48 to $10.42/10^6
   Btu. The meaning of these results and this range
   will become clear only after some detailed study and
   comparison with other published data. We would like
   to see the hydrogen cost from the computer program
   using the K-T assumptions. Using these assumptions,
   K-T presented a production cost of $4.95/10^6 Btu.

9. It is our opinion that the costs presented for
   hydrogen transmission are suitable for planning and
   intercomparison purposes when used in conjunction with
   the computer analysis. Storage costs for hydrogen
   have yet to be obtained.

10. We question the capital cost of the small plant as
    presented by K-T, and if the capital costs as presented
    by Winkler are scaled down from $1,200 \times 10^6$ SCF/day
    to 12.6×10^6 SCF/day, the cost will be $3.90 per daily
    SCF hydrogen, whereas Winkler reports $2. There is a
    factor of two difference in the capital cost per daily
    SCF of hydrogen as presented by Winkler and K-T.

JET PROPULSION LABORATORY *California Institute of Technology • 4800 Oak Grove Drive, Pasadena, California 91103*

July 17, 1979

Refer to: AAE-345-79-45:KRE:ecr

Dr. James E. Funk,
Associate Vice President
Academic Affairs
University of Kentucky
Lexington, KY 40506

Dear Dr. Funk:

Subject: "Hydrogen From Coal", Cost Estimation Seminar, (June 11-15, 1979)

Firstly, may I apologize for the lateness in submitting my comments to you on the
"Cost Estimation Seminar on Hydrogen from Coal" held in Provo, Utah.

My review and comments on the material presented are as follows:

General

Producing hydrogen from coal is a viable and proven process. The technology has
been around for a number of years as attested by the large number of small to
medium sized plants already built and in operation. But with the extremely
large complex plants now being proposed, many unknowns become evident which are
very cost sensitive, such as scale-up to much larger and complicated process
equipment, the integration of multiple trains of process and auxiliary equipment,
and the formulation of accurate variable as well as fixed operating and maintenance
costs.

Although the costs of the basic processes such as acid gas removal, CO shift, gas
purification and compression, and oxygen production are well founded and documented
the cost figures for the ancilliary processes are far from definitive and will
require a much greater depth of study and review. The magnitude of underestimating
these cost variables could easily be low by 25 to 50%. Because these cost figures
are substantially order-of-magnitude numbers, it is very dangerous to use them as
absolute numbers. They should be utilized only for cost comparisons of the various
technologies and processes and for preliminary developing of financing and cost
payout exercises. Included below are a number of project and process parameters
which should be more closely and definitively defined before they can be wholly
integrated into the overall plant investment and production costs.

148

1. <u>Capital costs</u> - Because of the extremely large size and complexity of the process equipment, a more accurate analysis of their manufactured cost should be made since many of the other design parameters such as piping, instrumentation, electrical, concrete, civil, painting and insulation are factored from these numbers.

2. By-Product costs and values for steam, sulfur, carbon dioxide, oxygen and nitrogen should be more definitively appraised as they are quite significant.

3. Items such as environmental requirements and costs, waste treatment and solids disposal, offsites and miscellaneous facilities such as roads, buildings, shops, laboratories, (which can be high as 20% of plant investment), coal preparation, transportation costs and storage of hydrogen should be given a much closer look.

4. Variable and fixed operating and maintenance costs should be more accurately defined.

5. Because of much higher temperatures and pressures being considered, a more detailed assessment should be made with regards to the metallurgical problems which will be encountered not only from pressure-temperature conditions but also the inevitable up and down cycling associated with multiple trains during startup periods and normal operating.

6. Construction time and startup periods of process units will be longer and drawn out due to the complexity of the fully integrated plants and could weigh heavily on projected cost forecasts. Escalation costs, during construction for materials and labor could be very significant.

7. Lastly, contingency funds should be very carefully analyzed both from the project and process standpoints. With the new and untried technologies involved, there is a real uncertainty in the design and manufactured cost of commercial-scaled equipment. In addition, as project design becomes more detailed and firm, considerable design changes will become necessary resulting in additional equipment and sometimes major changes in process control instrumentation and electrical.

I enjoyed being part of your review group and look forward to working with you again.

Respectfully,

K. R. Ekman
Member of Technical Staff

xc: C. England
J. Hanson
J. Kelley
G. Varsi

www.ingramcontent.com/pod-product-compliance
Lightning Source LLC
Chambersburg PA
CBHW020614270326
41927CB00005B/328